Gordon Marino

KIERKEGAARD IN THE PRESENT AGE

Preface by

Philip Rieff

MARQUETTE
UNIVERSITY

PRESS

MARQUETTE STUDIES IN PHILOSOPHY
No. 27
SERIES EDITOR, ANDREW TALLON

Library of Congress Cataloging-in-Publication Data

Marino, Gordon Daniel, 1952-
  Kierkegaard in the present age / Gordon Daniel Marino ;
preface by Philip Rieff.
      p. cm. — (Marquette studies in philosophy ; no. 27)
Includes bibliographical references and index.
  ISBN 0-87462-604-8 (pbk. : alk. paper)
1. Kierkegaard, Søren, 1813-1855. I. Title.
II. Marquette studies in philosophy ; # 27.
  B4377 .M37 2001
  198'.9—dc21

                                        2001007000

MARQUETTE UNIVERSITY PRESS
MILWAUKEE

The Association of Jesuit University Presses

CONTENTS

Preface by Philip Rieff 7

Acknowledgments 8

Dedication 9

Foreword 11

1. The Objective Thinker Is a Suicide 17

2. Is Madness Truth, Is Fanaticism Faith? 29

3. The Place of Reason in Kierkegaard's Ethics 43

4. Did Kierkegaard Believe in a Life after Death? 61

5. Can We Come to Psychoanalytic Terms with Death? ... 77
6. Kierkegaard contra Freud:
   On the Proper Scope of Our Moral Aspirations 83

7. Making the Darkness Visible:
   On the Distinction between Despair and Depression in
   Kierkegaard's *Journals* 99

Bibliography 113

Index 123

Author Biography 125

PREFACE

Gordon Marino is one of the world's leading Kierkegaard scholars. He is the basso profundo of Kierkegaard's war against the umwelt of the Church. His lyrical gift, as a Kierkegaard scholar, bears comparison to that of Professor Sir Laurence Olivier's trumpet voice as he calls down the wrath of God upon the French. The Church are Olivier's French. Gordon Marino is best read, in Olivier's voice, on his knees, praying to the god of battles for victory at Agincourt. Kierkegaard experiences Agincourt after Agincourt. He is the world's greatest writer as loser. Marino understands this and gives no quarter.

It is a paradox that would have delighted S.K. that this great Kierkegaard scholar was also the boxing coach at the Virginia Military Institute. Egyptomania is not Kierkegaard's condition of despair; nor is it Marino's.

Philip Rieff
Benjamin Franklin Professor of Sociology
& University Professor Emeritus
University of Pennsylvania

ACKNOWLEDGEMENTS

When I was a graduate student, Philip Rieff took special care to point out all the train wrecks of relationships in the academic life. He taught me that we scholars are an ambitious if not narcissistic lot, often willing to sacrifice a spouse, child, or entire family for a book. I thank him for constantly reminding me that even within the sphere of my own life, there are many more important matters than this book. Beatrice Beebe ran tireless interference with my tireless demons. If it were not for her, this book would never have received the importance in my life that it deserved. I am grateful to Alastair Hannay, Paul Holmer, Gene Outka, Philip Rieff, Vanessa Rumble, and Stephen Toulmin for discussing sections of this manuscript with me. I thank Andrew Tallon for his discernment and great patience and Cleo Granneman, Charles Grell, and Matthew Peterson for their assistance in bringing this manuscript into final form. Finally and eternally, I thank my wife, Susan Ellis Marino, for her gentle and steadfast instruction in the works of love.

Earlier versions of most of the essays that comprise this book appeared in journal format. "The Objective Thinker is a Suicide" appeared in *Philosophy Today* (1985). "Is Madness Truth is Fanaticism Faith" appeared in *The International Journalf or the Philosophy of Religion* (1987). The first version of "The Place of Reason in Kierkegaard's Ethics" was published in *Kierkegaardiana* (1996). "Did Kierkegaard Believe in a Life after Death" is the result of reworking "Salvation: a Reply to Harrison Hall" *Inquiry* (1984). "Can we Come to Psychoanalytic Terms with Death," first appeared in *Inquiry* (1984). The journal *Soundings* (1994) published my first attempt at, "Kierkegaard Contra Freud: On the Proper Scope of our Moral Aspirations."

This book is dedicated to that

most dedicated of teachers,

Philip Rieff

Foreword

As freshman scribblers we were all inculcated with the belief that we should stay away from the use of the first person pronoun. It went without saying that we were not to bring our own lives, our own concrete histories into our philosophical exercises. Though it took some time, Kierkegaard disabused me of the idea that it is impossible to take philosophical soundings in the first person.

No thanks to the classes that I was taking, I first began to take Kierkegaard seriously as a graduate student in philosophy in the late seventies. It was then, the heyday of analytic philosophy, and nearly every personally meaningful topic was *eo ipso* judged to be too unclear to be worthy of philosophical attention. The clarion call was for clarity of expression at any cost, even if it meant narrowing the field of inquiry to such a degree that there was little left to talk about, save the ordinary meanings of ordinary terms. I followed my professors in ignoring the Danish thinker, at least until the day when I encountered Kierkegaard afresh in a coffee shop.

At the time, I was going through a terrible divorce, to be sure, they are all terrible but at any rate, I was going through a terrible divorce and was slowly becoming unmoored. On seemingly permanent leave from graduate school, I was in my late twenties and too grief stricken to do much of anything. During the first few months after the break, people accepted my moping, but after two years my family and friends were becoming seriously concerned. Trying to stay one step ahead of my pain, I spent many afternoons in cafes. One of my favorite haunts was a combined coffee bar and bookstore. The book selection was thin and I had it more or less memorized, but one late November day, I spied a new volume, a brownish covered Harper edition of the Hong translation of Works *of Love*. By this time, I had become attracted to Kierkegaard by virtue of the fact that the titles of his books seemed to suggest that he was writing about topics that I had become a major in. I opened Works *of Love* to the first page. There was a passage from *Luke* that I politely ignored and immediately below it a page of commentary which, in one gust, toppled the fortress of cynicism that I lived in. The words that flung the door open were these:

> If it were true—as conceited shrewdness, proud of not being deceived, thinks—that one should believe nothing which he cannot see by means of his physical eyes, then first and foremost one ought to give up believing in love. If one did this and did it out of fear of being deceived, would not one then be deceived? Indeed, one can be deceived in many ways; one can be deceived in believing what is untrue, but on the other hand, one is also deceived in not believing what is true; one can be deceived by appearances, but one can also be deceived by the superficiality of shrewdness, by the flattering conceit which is absolutely certain that it cannot be deceived. Which deception is most dangerous? Whose recovery is more doubtful, that of him who does not see or of him who sees and still does not see? Which is more difficult, to awaken one who sleeps or to awaken one who, awake, dreams that he is awake? Which sight is more sorrowful, that which immediately and unrestrainedly moves to tears, like the sight of one unhappily deceived in love, or that which in a certain sense could tempt laughter, the sight of one who is self-deceived, whose foolish conceit of not being deceived is ludicrous, something to be laughed at, if its ludicrousness were not a still stronger expression for horror by signifying that he is not worth a tear? To cheat oneself out of love is the most terrible deception; it is an eternal loss for which there is no reparation, either in time or in eternity. [1]

I immediately bought the book and finished it by the next day. Kierkegaard's words worked important changes in me. For one, prior to my encounter with Works *of Love* and despite the fact that I was living in an age in which psychotherapy was regnant, I remained of the less than conscious opinion that psychological suffering had a stench about it. Being mentally tormented seemed to me to imply that you had failed in living. Kierkegaard's succor came in the form of assuring me that enduring psychological suffering was a meaningful activity that could be performed well or poorly. There was another lesson, one that I did not anticipate from the page gleaned in the coffee shop. In *Works of Love,* Kierkegaard brings a distinction to life between self-love and other love that had never visited me before. At that darkling time in my life, I was convinced that I loved the woman who had left me more than life itself. There was little that I was sure of but I was certain that I knew about love and that I was in love. I cannot now find the page with the message but somewhere in *Works of Love,* Kierkegaard seemed to whisper, "Well, young man, is it the woman or yourself that you love? If you love her so much then you ought to put her happiness before your own. And if she is better off without you, which even you have to acknowledge is a strong possibility, then you ought to be willing to part with her."

Today, orthodoxy has it that mental states are nothing but the echo of a chorus of neurotransmitters. Still, every now and then there comes along an idea which immediately turns our affective lives upside down. To me this suggests that meaning, not just molecules, play some role in determining our psychic states. The notion that truly loving someone might mean letting them go was for me one such transformative idea. The attitude that we take to our attitudes can make a great difference in our attitudes. With a nudge from Kierkegaard, my anguish took on a different cast or rather I was able to relate myself to it in a way that changed the anguish.

But, what has this confession to do with an otherwise scholarly study of Kierkegaard? A great deal. In contrast to my original academic sensibilities, Kierkegaard convinced me that serious and, for that matter, scholarly writing need not be synonymous with being objective and impersonal. A serious author is not necessarily one who can support his reading with 133 footnotes, or one who will not rest in his house-to-house scholarly fighting until he has backed his academic opponent into the corner of a self-contradiction. For Kierkegaard, a serious author is a concerned person who strives to speak to his reader in a meaningful way about meaningful issues.

This book represents a few of the lessons that I have taken from Kierkegaard in the course of my sentimental education. Some of them are old, penned in their original form as many as fifteen years ago. I offer them as an attempt to help bring Kierkegaard's thought to bear upon the present age. Much as he despised worldly judgment, the world has finally come to judge that Kierkegaard is a world historical thinker and, as such, he ought to be of something more than historical interest. Naive as it may sound, we ought to be able to learn something from him in the existential sense of that term.

In the first chapter, "The Objective Thinker is a Suicide," I present Kierkegaard's understanding of objectivity and attempt to explain the timely sense in which he judges the objective life posture to be a form of suicide. The opposite of objectivity is self-concern. The highest expression of self-concern is a concern for one's God relationship. But is the stress Kierkegaard places on this relationship an invocation to religious fanaticism? In the second chapter which, like the first, focuses upon *The Concluding Unscientific Postscript*, I will have Kierkegaard answer the charge that his call to faith is in fact a call to religious mania.

Some say that Kierkegaard underscores too strongly the subjective side of faith. The same has been said about his understanding of the moral life. One of the most important moral philosophers of the present age is Alasdair MacIntyre. His *After Virtue* is arguably one of the most influential moral treatises of the last twenty five years. In that seminal text, MacIntyre argues that when it came to ethics, Kierkegaard was much more than less an irrationalist who believed that passion itself was the ultimate arbiter of right and wrong. In chapter three, "On the Place of Reason in Kierkegaard's Ethics," I examine the relationship between reason and righteousness in Kierkegaard's writings.

In chapter four I return once again to Kierkegaardian questions concerning the forms of the life of faith. Following one line of Kierkegaard's thought, there has, of late, developed a tendency for Christians to believe that the content of faith is of little importance. More specifically, there is today within large circles of Christianity very little in the way of a requirement that the true believer believe in a life after death. Some prominent Kierkegaard scholars have come to the conclusion that Kierkegaard was simply too smart to believe in mumbo jumbo to the effect that death is not the end. In chapter four, I address the question, Do Kierkegaard's writings reflect a belief in an afterlife?

The next two chapters bring Kierkegaard into dialogue with Freud. Some will argue that Freud is going through still another death and that his writings are only of historical interest. It is my position that for all our dismissals of Freud, much of Freud's ethic has in fact become orthodoxy. In chapter five, "Can we Come to Psychoanalytic Terms with Death," I offer a Kierkegaardian response to the person who, like Freud, preaches that death is simply a part of life and that maturity requires that we accept as such and so without the sop of hope for an afterlife.

It does not require much percipience to note that people have, in some sense, become less stringent in their moral postures. Whether for good or for bad, we have developed a much more accepting attitude towards a host of common failings. There is a line of moral psychology that runs from Schopenhauer to Freud which claims that, for our own moral good, we ought to be more realistic in the moral demands that we place upon ourselves. In chapter six, "On the Proper Scope of our Moral Aspirations," I enlist Kierkegaard's answer to the question, Should the demands of conscience be leveled to psychological reality?

In the final chapter, "On Making the Darkness Visible: On the Distinction between Depression and Despair in Kierkegaard's Writings," I use Kierkegaard to help resuscitate a crucial distinction that has been effaced in the present age, namely, the distinction between psychological and spiritual illness.

Notes

[1] Kierkegaard, S. *Works of Love.* trans. Edna and Howard Hong. New York: Harper and Brothers, 1962, p. 23.

Chapter 1

The Objective Thinker Is a Suicide

1. Introduction

Dead. The objective individual is all but literally dead, or so says Søren Kierkegaard here and there throughout his many invocations to inwardness. There is no denying abstracted man's nominal existence, or to put it in Kierkegaard's own terms, that even he "also exists"—but that is the extent of it. Witness Kierkegaard's description of a lost child of that enduring age—the age of understanding. A suicide? Perhaps. It is not easy to say, death may be a matter of degree:

> Not even a suicide these days does away with himself in desperation but deliberates on this step so long and so sensibly that he is strangled by calculation, making it a moot point whether or not he can really be called a suicide, inasmuch as it was in fact the deliberating that took his life. A premeditated suicide he was not, but rather a suicide by means of premeditation.[1]

The inward individual lives by straining to give life to his guiding thought. Forgetting he exists the objective individual does half the same; he lives as though he were Thought itself. If he were true to his creed, he would finish the job and be done with existence. Witness these lines from Kierkegaard's philosophical *magnum opus*, the *Concluding Unscientific Postscript:*

> If in our day thinking had not become something strange, something secondhand, thinkers would indeed make a totally different impression on people, as was the case in Greece,

where a thinker was also an ardent existing person impassioned by his thinking, as was the case at one time in Christendom, where a thinker was a believer who ardently sought to understand himself in the existence of faith. If it were the same with thinkers in our day, pure thinking would have led to one suicide after another, because suicide is the only existence-consequence of pure thinking.[1]

Make no mistake about it, Kierkegaard is in earnest: the objective thinker dies from deliberation. But how, and in what sense? Kierkegaard's most detailed account of objectivity occurs in his *Concluding Unscientific Postscript* and it is to this text that we will look to resolve these questions.

2. A Caveat

The reader need not be told that there is more to Kierkegaard than what he found wanting in Hegel. Still, there is always a temptation to find nothing but the one in the other, and the subject matter of this essay is sure to amplify that temptation. After all, Kierkegaard's critique of objectivity is written in the most ironizing Hegelianese. And there is no mistaking the fact that the Absolute Idealist is the expressed target of hundreds of critical barbs.

Confusing thought and existence, the objective thinker has forgotten he exists, or so Kierkegaard complains. To be sure Kierkegaard deplores the version of this confusion as he finds it reflected in the canons of Speculative Philosophy. But much more than the reflected forms it is the many and variegated, unreflected forms, aptly termed by David Gouwens, the "diseases of reflection," that Kierkegaard sets out to treat. Kierkegaard held that for the existing individual, thought only exists as a possibility of existence.[2] The same holds for mistakes expressed in the medium of thought and so for mistaken philosophical doctrines. It is not the possible but the actual confusion that strings the bow of Kierkegaard's concern. Or again, it is not the abstractions that invite his reminders but the abstracted half-life of the individual who has forgotten he exists. This is not to deny the connection between possibility and actuality or in this case between abstraction and abstractedness; it is only to place them in the order in which Kierkegaard keeps them. The polemic against Hegel is there; nevertheless, Kierkegaard was no more concerned with razing theories than he was with writing them. It is the existing individual, the person at risk of spiritual, which is to say, actual suicide, that Kierkegaard is concerned with.

3. The Objective Thinker Is a Suicide

Johannes Climacus, the pseudonymous author of the *Concluding Unscientific Postscript,* states that the truth that is the aim of objectivity is a unity of thought and being *(Væren)*[3] to which the individual truth seeker is at best accidentally related. There are two media,[4] says Climacus, thought and existence. Unlike the Truth that is a way, namely, the one he calls "subjective," objective truth is written in the universal language of thought. Subjectively speaking, it is a person's passional relation to his thought that makes for verity. Objectively speaking, one can grasp the truth without being grasped by it; one's relation to his thought is of no objective consequence. Aristotle wrote the formula: the objective truth is a universal form in the universal mind.[5] Literally selfless, all-too-rational man chases after a truth that cares nothing for him.

Objective thought is indifferent to the individual and it is indifference that objective thought requires. The earmark of objectivity is disinterest.[6] This is not to say that abstracted man takes no interest in his abstractions;[7] quite the contrary, they own it all. The interest of the aesthete is always directed outward,[8] toward some object of higher or lower desire. True aesthete that he is, the objective thinker has the object of his thought to sink all self-concern in. While the inward individual thinks as though his eternal life hung upon the result, his objective counterpart settles for nothing less than a scientific insouciance.

Kierkegaard conceives consciousness *(Bevisthed)* to be a triadic relation,[9] the three poles of which are existence, the individual, and ideality. Unless they be assimilated into one's interest in his existence, no relation between existence and ideality[10] is established. Existence *(qua* immediacy) is simply passed over into ideality and that is the end of it. In Kierkegaard/Climacus's terms, there is no "collision" between these two realms, only a transition from the one into the other.[11] There is an awareness of an object of thought but none of the subject to which the object is really not related. John Elrod[12] is correct: for Kierkegaard there is no consciousness without self-consciousness, and no self-consciousness without self-concern. So long as the individual's interest in his existence is not engaged neither is he. Disinterested as he is the objective thinker is unselfconscious.

Unselfconscious as he is, the objective thinker assumes an absolute nonpositional perspective. As though situated on a transcendental *pou sto,* he looks back upon the world he is immersed in. Though a participant, he dreams he is a spectator.[13] Objectively speaking, the observer's point of view is an illusory one or so Kierkegaard could have argued. But an error in perspective is only a pecadillo in comparison with the other problems he diagnoses.

On virtually every one of his philosophical pages, Kierkegaard distinguishes between thought and existence. Though no theory is provided, it is patent that he takes ideality to be everything existence is not, namely, universal and unchanging. "But to exist," avers Climacus, "signifies first and foremost to be a particular individual"[14]—not thought. Second, whatever comes to be is by nature, always becoming[15]—not thought. Repetitively, Climacus indites, "existence is movement."[16]

In that fecund but unfinished text, *De Omnibus Dubitandum Est,* objective thinking[17] is portrayed as a disinterested process of putting existence into contact with ideality.[18] The result is the possibility of a relation.[19] As previously noted, the actual relation, consciousness, is identified with the *"inter-esse"*[20] that objectivity disallows. Objective thinking describes existence in terms of ideality: where the description fits, the objective truth is. But it never does.

A skeptic cut from Humean cloth, Kierkegaard rejects the essentialism that might find sense and stability in change. The flux of existence cannot be fixed in the fixing terms of thought. Abrogate[21] and where the existing individual is not concerned, approximate[22]—that is the worst and best that thought can do with existence. While Kierkegaard acknowledges that ideality can be brought into existence, both he and Climacus are emphatic—

there is no going in the other direction: existence cannot be thought.

> Existence, like motion, is a very difficult matter to handle. If I think it, I cancel it, and then I do not think it. It would seem correct to say that there is something that cannot be thought—namely, existing.[23]

> The only *an sich* which cannot be thought is existing, with which thinking has nothing at all to do.[24]

Represented in abstract terms, the flux is found a frozen object of thought. Again, movement is of the essence, which is to say, actuality, of existence. Idealized, this movement is nullified. Process is misunderstood as a result; that which is always and freely becoming is written up as a tentatively concluded determinate something. The cognitive subject reaches for the essence, but grasps only the possibility of existence.

> Only by annulling actuality *[Virkelighed]*[25] can abstraction grasp it, but to annul it is precisely to change it into possibility.[26]

"All knowledge about actuality is possibility,"[27] and so we have it once again—existence is unthinkable. But is this what Kierkegaard/Climacus means when he censures the objective thinker for having forgotten what it means to exist?[28] In the end, forgetfulness is not just a matter of existence being beyond the ken of cognitive relations. There must be some way of remembering existence that disinterested thinking dooms us to forget. If existence cannot be grasped at all then why the reproach for having forgotten it? It is not objective knowledge that is the Lethe but unthinking devotion to it. More to Kierkegaard's axial point, the actuality of existence is appropriated in the same passionate self-concern that objectivity annuls.

Once more, all knowledge about reality is possibility and all our relations with reality are epistemic, save one:

> The only actuality concerning which an existing person has more than knowledge about is his own actuality, that he exists, and this actuality is his absolute interest.[29]

Unlike thought, interest understands existence in and as process. It is in this sense that being concerned about oneself is something more than a cognitive relation. Thought contents have little to do with it—understanding existence is existing with a passionate and personal interest in your own existence.

Kierkegaard comes very close to identifying passion and self-concern but there is an important difference. Though an infinite and personal interest is a passion *(Lidenskab)* there are passions that have none of the self-consciousness of self-concern. As we will see in chapter two, the fanatic is a case in point.[30] Nevertheless, passion is essential. Given the equation of consciousness and interest, being conscious is, in part, existing passionately. The other part is, as it were, the direction of that passion, the truth that is a passionate personal concern about one's existence and not about one or another objective truth claim. In the lines preceding those registered below, Climacus is weighing different strategies for inciting passion. Having considered two examples almost identical to this, the third, he writes:

> [I]f a Pegasus and an old nag were hitched to a carriage for a driver not usually disposed to passion and he was told: Now drive—I think it would be successful. And this is what existing is like if one is to be conscious of it.[31]

As soon as the driver recognizes the horses that are pulling his trap he is possessed of a desire to take charge and steer his fate. Both the particularity and process of existence are expressed in this intention. Thought is and finds in everything a result.[32] Unlike it, concern walks along with existence as a continuous striving process.[33] This is certainly and perfectly imaged in Climacus's reluctant driver. Offering a reading of his own text our author continues:

> Eternity is infinitely quick like that winged steed, temporality is an old nag, and the existing person is the driver, that is, if existing is not to be what people usually call existing, because then the existing person is no driver but a drunken peasant who lies in the wagon and sleeps and lets the horses shift for themselves. Of course, he also drives, he is also a driver, and likewise there perhaps are many who—also exist.[34]

For Kierkegaard and all the authors he dances on to his stage, the individual is a synthesis of, *inter alia*, time and eternity.[35] A person realizes[36] the synthesis that he is by taking a passionate interest in his existence, not by abstracting from it.

There is a driver who really drives and another who only does so by default. It is the same with individual existence. In a sentence-long preface to the brace of passages cited above, Climacus quips, "Existing, if this is not to be understood as just any sort of existing, cannot be done without passion."[37] Prescinding passion from thought and almost always[38] thinking, the objective person exists in the same loose sense that the besotted, dozing peasant drives.

The distinction between real and nominal existence is carried over into the next paragraph. Here the epistemological trappings are removed and the 'existence is movement' thesis cast in a new light:

> Inasmuch as existence is motion, it holds true that there is indeed a continuity that holds the motion together, because otherwise there is no motion.[39]

On first inspection, it seems as though continuity must be intrinsic to existence. After all, if there were no continuity, there would be no movement. And yet Climacus stresses "the difficulty for the existing person is to give existence the continuity without which everything just disappears."[40] If continuity were there from the beginning, the need to establish it would not arise. But it does.

In the Interlude to his *Philosophical Fragments,* Climacus contends that while being is never becoming, existence always is. If, then, the existing individual is to have some share of being, there must be something unchanging about him. There must be continuity.[41] Climacus affirms that by virtue of our being embodied each of us "also exists"; but physical or, for that matter, mental continuity is a far cry from the human being that he keeps calling us to.[42]

For someone who is not taking him in precisely the right sense, Kierkegaard's solution comes as something of a surprise. The ballast is to come from ideality. Though it cannot be thought, "existence puts it together in this way: the one who is thinking is existing."[43] The individual is a protean denizen of a protean world; nevertheless, he is potentially related to something outside the flux. He must bring the outside in. The difficulty of bringing continuity into existence "lies in joining this definite something and the ideality of thinking by willing to think it."[44]

Continuity in existence does not come by abstracting from existence. So long as I walk this earth I cannot fly off into the heaven of ideas. I cannot become what I think nor can I become pure Reason itself.[45] If thought is to penetrate existence the individual must make it his purpose. He has an idea of the Good; let him strive to inscribe it in the medium of his existence. If he succeeds (in striving, that is) he earns his *telos*. Thought enters existence as a unifying purpose.

By lines of implication the certainty attaching to one claim can be passed along to others. One proposition is the logical, which is to say, automatic consequence of another. Noticing this, or perhaps simply confusing knowledge and existence, some conclude that with the right mental representations everything else, wisdom and virtue included, will follow thoughtlessly along. Kierkegaard/Climacus contravenes: continuity in existence does not come as the mechanical result of anything. If at all, continuity, comes from continual moral striving. And it is the individual's interest in his existence that stimulates this activity. Climacus writes, "For the existing person, existing is for him his highest interest, and his interestedness in existing is his actuality,"[46] i.e., the continuity in his existence.

Though not in the "essentially human, ethico-religious sphere" Kierkegaard acknowledges that there are subject matter for which a disinterested treatment is entirely fitting.[47] However, when the suppression of self-concern becomes chronic and the objective thinker objectified, Kierkegaard calls it suicide. And when he remarks that the child of the age *dies from deliberation,* he ought to be taken at his word. The objective individual does away with the interest that is his reality. And what is the term for someone who does away with his reality? A suicide.

But why suicide? Why the suppression of the self-concern that is the core of the self? While this question is fare for another essay, a few proleptic lines are, I think, in order. Kierkegaard instructs that the self concern which finds fruition in faith leads us into sacrifices and forms of self-concern that our lower nature does not much care for. Once more, Kierkegaard often writes as though we all have some innate sense that if we resolve to follow Him Christ is sure to lead us into dangerous places. But for those who would prefer their Kierkegaard without the constant references to Jesus, our author observes, "Man has made a discovery... the way to make life easy is to make it meaningless."[48] The way to make life meaningless is to strangle the self-concern that animates the question of meaning but that again is a form of spiritual which is to say actual suicide.

NOTES

[1] Søren Kierkegaard, *Two Ages*, trans. Howard and Edna Hong (Princeton: Princeton University Press, 1978), 68-69 (VIII 65) (Note: following every Hong edition page is the page reference of the quote or section from the Danish 1st edition or the *Papirer*). Unless otherwise stated, textual references are to Søren Kierkegaard's *Concluding Unscientific Postscript*, trans. and ed. Howard and Edna Hong (Princeton: Princeton University Press, 1992). 308 (VII 264); see also 342 (VII 296-297).

[2] 316 (VII 271-272), 317 (VII 272-273).

[3] 189-190 (VII 157-158).

[4] 313-314 (VII 269).

[5] See *De Anima* 430a14, 432a2-4.

[6] 37 (VII 26), 314 (VII 270) *passim.*; see also Søren Kierkegaard, *Johannes Climacus* (also known as *De Omnibus Dubitandum Est*), trans. Howard and Edna Hong (Princeton: Princeton University Press, 1985), 170-172 (IV B 1 148-IV B 1 150).

[7] 21 (VII 11-12).

[8] 37 (VII 26). In this sense there is something objective about the artist and poet. Hence Kierkegaard's footnote:

> Art and poetry have been called anticipations of the eternal. If one desires to speak in this fashion, one must nevertheless note that art and poetry are not essentially related to an existing individual; for their contemplative enjoyment, the joy over what is beautiful, is disinterested, and the spectator of the work of art is contemplatively outside himself *qua* existing individual. (313 [VII 269])

[9] Kierkegaard, *Johannes Climacus* 169-170 (IV B 1 148).

[10] Kierkegaard, *Johannes Climacus* 170 (IV B 1 148).

[11] Kierkegaard, *Johannes Climacus* 168 (IV B 1 147), 170 (IV B 1 148).

[12] John W. Elrod, *Being and Existence in Kierkegaard's Pseudonymous Works* (Princeton: Princeton University Press, 1975), 50-51.

[13] 132 (VII 107), 159 (VII 131) *passim.*

[14] 326 (VII 281); see also 330 (VII 285).

[15] 73 (VII 56), 86 (VII 67) *passim;* see also Søren Kierkegaard, *Philosophical Fragments,* trans. Howard and Edna Hong (Princeton: Princeton University Press, 1974), 90f (IV 253).

[16] 264 (VII 232), 309 (VII 265) *passim.*

[17] Kierkegaard, *Johannes Climacus* 170 (IV B 1 146). In *Johannes Climacus* it is clear that Kierkegaard meant to identify 'objective thinking' with 'reflection.'

[18] "Objective," "abstract thinking," and "reflection" also applies to excogitations that treat only the relations between ideas.

[19] Kierkegaard, *Johannes Climacus* 167 (IV B 1 146), 169 (IV B 1 148).

[20] "Consciousness," writes Kierkegaard, "is relationship, and it brings with it interest or concern; a duality which is perfectly expressed with pregnant double meaning by the word 'interest'" (Latin *inter-esse,* meaning (I) "to be between," (ii) "to be a matter of concern") (Kierkegaard, *Johannes Climacus* 170 (IV B 1 148)); see also Kierkegaard's *Concluding Unscientific Postscript* 315 (VII 271) and Kierkegaard's *Eighteen Upbuilding Discourses,* trans. Howard and Edna Hong (Princeton: Princeton University Press, 1990), 233 (IV 123).

[21] 118 (VII 97), 308 (VII 264), 317 (VII 272).

[22] 224 (VII 188), 190 (VII 158) *passim.*

[23] 308-309 (VII 264).

[24] 328 (VII 283).

[25] The Danish term *'Virkelighed'* can be rendered either 'reality' or 'actuality.'

[26] 314-315 (VII 270).

[27] 316 (VII 271).

[28] 93 (VII 74). 249 (VII 210) *passim.*

[29] 316 (VII 271); see also 317 (VII 272), 331 (VII 285).

[30] 33 (VII 22), 36 (VII 25), 193f (VII 161f).

[31] 311-312 (VII 267).

[32] 33-34 (VII 21-24), 73 (VII 54) *passim.*

[33] 121 (VII 99).

[34] 312 (VII 267).

[35] 55 (VII 43), 82 (VII 63) *passim.*

[36] 'Realize' is intended in both the cognitive and existential sense of the term.

[37] 311 (VII 267).

[38] I say "almost" because S.K. writes, "When it is impossible to think existence, and the existing individual nevertheless thinks, what does this signify? It signifies that he thinks intermittently... (329 (VII 283)).

[39] 312 (VII 267). The Swenson translation (trans. David F. Swenson and Walter F. Lowrie (Princeton: Princeton University Press, 1968)) renders this quote differently, and I think a bit more clearly. It reads, "Insofar as existence consists in movement there must be something which can give continuity to the movement and hold it together, for otherwise there is no movement" (277).

[40] 312 (VII 267).

[41] Kierkegaard express this thought poignantly: "...when people who have fantastically dabbled in everything, have been everything possible, one day in concern ask the pastor whether they will actually remain the same in the beyond—after they have not been able in this life to endure being the same for a fortnight, and therefore have gone through all kinds of transmutations" (176 (VII 146)).

[42] Søren Kierkegaard, *Either/Or, Volume I,* trans. Howard and Edna Hong (Princeton: Princeton University Press, 1987), 64-65 (I 47-48).

[43] 309 (VII 264).

[44] 169 (VII 140), 308 (VII 264) *passim.*

[45] 93 (VII 73), 329 (VII 284).

[46] 314 (VII 270).

[47] 92 (VII 73), 193 (VII 161); also Kierkegaard's *Johannes Climacus* 152 (IV B 1 134).

[48] *Søren Kierkegaard's Journals and Papers,* trans. and ed. Howard and Edna Hong, assist. by Gregor Malantschuck (Bloomington: Indiana University Press, 1975), 3:346 entry 2993 (XI^2 A 127 *n.d.*, 1854).

CHAPTER 2

IS MADNESS TRUTH,
IS FANATICISM FAITH?

I

In the second section of his *Concluding Unscientific Postscript*,[1] Kierkegaard launches a frontal assault on the beachhead of objectivity. Speaking in the sacral language of argument, he threads a line of thought that stretches from the Ancient Greek Skeptics through Hume. Whatever comes to be (exist) is always becoming. Ideas describe things in their own static terms and so they cannot help but misunderstand or to use Kierkegaard's phrase, "abrogate existence." If, as Kierkegaard defines it, truth is the identity of thought and being,[2] then we must agree—in a world where being is replaced by existence there are no truths, only approximations.[3]

The ontological incompatibility that leads to this skeptical result would be enough to stop any truly abstracted thinker in his tracks, but Kierkegaard presses on. Posing an amended version of the objective problem (what is truth?), he self-inquires, "What is my, Søren Kierkegaard's, relation to the truth?" The answer is not long in coming—"subjectivity is truth" (*Subjektiviteten er Sandheden*)![4]

The truth that Kierkegaard limns is a passional relation between an individual and his thought content. Existence, human and otherwise, is a movement. For the existing human being there can be no results. The truth is a way, a movement with direction, a self-directed struggle to live up to an ideal. According to

Kierkegaard's unobjective criterion, truth is not a property of ideas but of the individual's commitment to them. This commitment comes neither from habit nor calculation but from passion.

To be sure, Kierkegaard wrote to kindle a spark in the withered souls of the systematically abstracted. Still, the accent on pathos often rings extreme. Where truth is concerned, is a fiery spirit enough? Is the objective thought content really a matter of indifference? The author of the *Postscript* is quite explicit, better to be passionately wed to a false idea than dispassionately wed to one that hits its referential mark. Consider this pair of well-traveled sentences:

> If someone who lives in the midst of Christianity enters, with knowledge of the true idea of God, the house of God, the house of the true God, and prays, but prays in untruth, and if someone lives in an idolatrous land but prays with all the passion of infinity, although his eyes are resting upon the image of an idol—where, then, is there more truth? The one prays in truth to God although he is worshipping an idol; the other prays in untruth to the true God and is therefore in truth worshiping an idol.[5]

These lines deserve what they will get, namely, a closer reading, but for now it is enough to record the terms of the contrast. One worshipper is possessed of the right idea and wrong spirit, the other has it the other, preferred way around—right spirit, wrong idea.

In the heat of Kierkegaard's dialectical diatribes, pathos looms more and more important. Page after page, Kierkegaard's reader begins to misunderstand—passion equals subjectivity, inwardness, and truth. The truth that Kierkegaard has in heart and mind is, of course, an ethico-religious one, necessarily spelt with an uppercase tee. This, however, does not spare him from the potentially embarrassing fact that there is a passion in madness that is hard to outstrip.

But has Kierkegaard's penchant for paradox taken him so far that he would have us call the ravings of a psychotic 'truth'? Would he have all truth seekers apply for a term of study in a lunatic asylum? I do not believe so, but let it never be said that Kierkegaard shrinks from such repugnant thoughts. Quite the contrary, Johannes Climacus, the pseudonymous author of the *Postscript* remarks that in a purely subjective sense "lunacy and truth are ultimately indistinguishable."[6] This confession comes as no surprise to the misguided reader who begins with the presupposition that Kierkegaard was an ardent irrationalist. Just the same, Kierkegaard seems to have taken himself aback, for in a footnote he adds this disclaimer:

> Even this is not true, however, because madness never has the inwardness of infinity. Its fixed idea is a kind of objective something, and the contradiction of madness lies in wanting to embrace it with passion.[7]

Once more, all knowledge is half-truth (approximation), and all vehicles of knowledge, i.e., thoughts, are finite approximation-objects. The apparent contradiction that is madness stems from the disproportion between a virtually infinite passion and its finite approximation-object. The inwardness of the infinite is an infinite interest in one's existence. All too easily confused with vanity, this self-concern finds its natural and true voice in a boundless yearning for infinitude. More to the less abstract point, the individual who loves himself as he ought to love his neighbor longs for his God. This longing is the unselfish self-love that Kierkegaard calls us to, and the individual in whom it abides leaps for the ever-unchanging by striving to bring his existence into relation with an ideal. Whether or not his guiding thought be a faithful image of impersonal reality makes no subjective difference. All pathos is concentrated in the individual's relation to his thought, not the thought (approximation-object) itself.[8]

No matter how cherished an ideal may be, there is no becoming it. In terms of the *Fragments*,[9] it is as simple as Kierkegaard's version of Aristotle's metaphysics. Being is never becoming and whatever comes into existence cannot come to be that which is never becoming. For the purposes of this argument or play on one, ideality is a form of being (unchanging existence), and so for Kierkegaard I repeat - there is no becoming what one thinks.[10] For Aristotle it is a complex matter of habit, not for Kierkegaard. The individual who aims to bring his thought into existence works against the flux. Here the incommensurability of madness is nowhere to be found. The relating activity that is the being qua continuity of human existence is a continuous (unchanging) effort expressing a continuous (infinite) interest in one's existence.

False worshipper that he is likely to be, the objective thinker supposes that there is nothing more to being in truth than being possessed of true conceptions. Equally cocksure, the madman does not trouble about relating his existence to an ideal. The personal relation to the eternal that madness flees from despairing about is carefully left aside. Consciously or un-, the madman turns all self-concern out. Gone is the self-knowledge of care. Gone, too, is the gentleness of longing. In some fixed and fixing idea the inwardness of the infinite is brought to a finite point. The passion of madness is a passionate insistence upon the objective truth claims of some lunatic idea. Whether it be Plato's ideas or Tom O'bedlam's makes no essential difference; so long as the object of deflected self-interest is just that, an object over and against the self,[11] interest—and for Kierkegaard that means consciousness[12]—is objectified, limited, and ultimately finite.

Clearly the delusional thought content is not the problem or at least not the abyss. The way the madman has lost is a way of relating to the eternal, not a way of conceiving it. The religious fanatic is a case in this sad point. Kierkegaard teaches that faith and truth amount to one another and to inwardness alike. Here the terms that Kierkegaard interchanges are exchanged; as madness falls short of truth, fanaticism falls short of faith.

No less than his irreligious counterpart, the religious madman has what the age lacks, and to the limited extent that thought can represent God, the absolute subject, as object, he has the right approximation-object; but mind you, the false worshipper has the same. Kierkegaard is descanting upon the hopes and fears of a burgeoning field of biblical criticism. The objective problem is raised. We have received the Word; now, can anyone establish that it is true? Of course not, Kierkegaard insists, "for nothing is more readily evident than that the greatest attainable certainty with respect to anything historical is merely an approximation."[13]

The objective approach to Christianity is not merely doomed; it is spiritual suicide. Self-concern, the most frequent definiens of

Kierkegaard's countless definitions of faith is "the subject's personal, infinite, impassioned interestedness."[14] Objectification requires the suppression or at least deflection of this interest. The cost could not be steeper if Beelzebub fixed it himself:

> [H]appiness inheres precisely in the infinite, personal, impassioned interestedness, and it is precisely this that one relinquishes in order to become objective. . .[15]

The absent-minded individual that Kierkegaard so tirelessly pasquinades is painted as such a bloodless figure that he needs to be officially reminded when he has at last, literally passed away.[16] Do not, however, be misled by Climacus' caricatures; Kierkegaard did not require his modern critics to point out that abstracted man has a genuine passion for abstract thought. But as both the madman and fanatic reveal, it is not passion that objectivity disallows but personal interest. Still, treating the objective approach, Climacus considers the New Testament scholar whose life is his scholarly work. Enter one image of the fanatic:

> To be infinitely interested in relation to that which at its maximum always remains only an approximation is a self-contradiction and thus is comical. If passion is posited nevertheless, zealotism ensues. Every iota is of infinite value for the infinitely interested passion. The fault inheres not in the infinitely interested passion but in this, that its object has become an approximation-object.[17]

So long as an object is the interest, the interest is an impersonal one; and so long as the interest is impersonal, the mode is objective—passion or no. One might go further, and the author of the *Postscript* seems to, for in a footnote Kierkegaard intimates that within every actually infinite interest a searching spirit lurks. Where nothing is a matter of indifference; "The objective point of view is hereby also reduced *in adsurdum*, and subjectivity is posited."[18] In other words, if the interest is really infinite, it is also personal. A few lines above those cited below, Kierkegaard observes that there was something more than the risible in the letter fanaticism of by-gone days. Even though it assumed an obsessive, ostensibly objective form, there was, at bottom, a gnawing spiritual concern. As Climacus explains it, medieval

theologians went through their intellectual paces with the expectation that their labor would, or at least could, yield a result for
faith. While these hopes bespeak a certain error, it is a peccadillo
compared with the ignorance that is passionlessness. At any rate,
the critics are not so fatuous these days, or so Kierkegaard might
as well wryly note:

> Although attacks are still being made on the Bible, although
> learned theologians defend it linguistically and critically, this
> entire procedure is now partly antiquated; and above all
> precisely because one becomes more and more objective, one
> does not have in mind the crucial conclusions with regard to
> faith.[19]

The longing that is the fanatic's kernel of faith does not take
seed in more gnarled forms of pseudo-religious mania. Indeed,
where Kierkegaard praises passion and not so indirectly lashes the
age, read with caution—the zealot is apt to be cast in a more
favorable light than Kierkegaard thinks he deserves. Perhaps there
is a distinction to be drawn between the zealot and the overly
zealous but distinction or not, there is indeed a Kierkegaardian
perspective on fanaticism that robs it of the innocence and truth
that some remarks suggest.

2

> . . .but if the uncertainty which is the mark and form of faith
> ceases, then we have not advanced in religiousness but have
> relapsed to childish forms. As soon as uncertainty is not the
> form of certitude, as soon as uncertainty does not continually
> keep the religious person hovering in order continually to
> grasp certitude, as soon as certainty seals with lead, as it were,
> the religious person—well, then he is naturally about to
> become part of the mass.[20]

Kierkegaard never contradicts Climacus' oft repeated claim
that faith is a passionate clinging to something objectively uncertain.[21] Actually, "uncertain" is too cozy a term. Kierkegaard goes
further and calls Christianity "absurd," "an offense to reason."
Even the most virile terms can be penned into the pulp of patois.
It is enough to acknowledge that the articles of faith are mighty

hard to believe. Some would and do say something more. On a
positively burning page Freud indites:

> The whole thing is so patently infantile, so foreign to reality,
> that to anyone with a friendly attitude toward humanity it is
> painful to think that the great majority of mortals will never
> be able to rise above this view of life.[22]

Kierkegaard's ideal type appreciates the logic but clings to the
incertitude just the same, that is, against his better, this-worldly
judgement.

The objective uncertainty that is the object of faith must be
recognized for what it is, namely, an uncertainty and worse. But
has the gadfly who set out to make essential things hard, and so
possible, rendered them fantastic and impossible?[23] After all,
there is no deciding to think things are the way they are not. But
that is not the requirement; faith considered as a commitment, as
a consciously holding to, sets itself apart from propositional
belief.

Facing the light, turn the ideal in another direction and there
you have it, the infinitely passionate commitment is decisiveness;[24] or the same problem again, faith is the decision to believe.
And what does it mean to believe? Something more than checking
off sentence tokens as true, that much is certain. For the most
part, belief blindly obeys the dictates of an image of reason. No
act of will is required in order to stamp the claims that come with
this imprimatur's approval. Conviction follows argument as a
matter of course. The individual's relation to his thought content
is thoughtlessly decided by an impersonal assessment of the
relation between said thoughts and reality at large. If the idea
corresponds and/or coheres, he is automatically behind it; if not,
then not.

Kierkegaard is firm, reason cannot close the gap that faith must
leap, for with the gap goes the possibility of faith. There is no
practical reasoning up to the highest good, no intellectual creep-
ing up to God. There is no objective exemption from the
subjective task. Mind you, Climacus warns:

> And here it must be regarded as perdition's illusion (which has
> remained ignorant of the fact that the decision is rooted in

subjectivity) or as an equivocation of illusiveness (which
shoves off the decision by objective treatment in which there
is no decision in all eternity) to assume that this transition
from something objective to a subjective acceptance follows
directly of its own accord, since precisely this is the decisive
point and an objective acceptance (*sit venia verbo* [pardon the
expression]) is paganism or thoughtlessness.[25,26]

Progress has been made; it is only the rarest of fools who expects
his faith to fall from either the bottom of a syllogism or the final
page of some forthcoming New Testament study. Still, there are
many ways of proof seeking. If it is not an ontological argument,
the fanatic has the irrefragable evidence of a conversion experience or, if not that, then some positively maniacal understanding of the Scriptures. In any case, the particular path to certitude
is not the source of the misguided direction. The fanatic may or
may not have his reasons - it makes no essential difference. No
more than reason, corybantic insistence cannot close the gap that
faith must leap, for with the gap goes faith.

Despite what Kierkegaard's personae could not lead Kierkegaard
to believe, Pascal of north and south agree, "without risk there is
no faith."[27] Let us never forget, for parroting the phrase, the leap
of faith leaves the only known world behind.[28] In the end, and well
before, Kierkegaard could see that if faith is following in
You-Know-Whose tracks, then it is also suffering. Is it any
wonder then that such a flock of formulae exist for removing the
risk? One strategy instructs, if you must die to this world, devalue
it first. Paint the aesthetic life as a bauble, or better yet as death
itself, and you are off. If there is nothing to lose, there is no risk;
but for the stoic no less than proof-seeker, Kierkegaard repeats,
"without risk there is no faith." Every fanatic's well-trodden path
is another popular way around. Here one need only imagine that
the logos has become scientific theory. According to the corresponding fantasy, if Christianity is true, and one knows, believes,
or at least pounds his fist about it, then he is most certainly a
Christian. Once more, the absolute untruth that the right ideal
equals the right spirit.

Where there is no risk there may be calculation, but no choice,
no decisiveness, in the stringent Kierkegaardian sense. Second

step, where there is certainty, there is no risk. Heaven knows, there is certainty enough in fanaticism, hence there is no risk, no decisiveness, and, alas, no faith.[29] Scholium: where there is certainty, justified or un-, there is no need of trust, and where there is no need, there is no trust. There is no passionately cleaving to objective certitudes. What we think we know we are safe to forget. The ever-present awareness that is the passionate and personal relation that both Climacus and his creator insist upon can never be fulfilled by head-nodding acts of intellectual assent. Inject the passion of madness and it makes no difference. Remember, a true conception is not nearly enough and, passion or no, "...an objective assessment of Christianity *(sit venia verbo)* is paganism or thoughtlessness." Again, as the Greek does in fact suggest, Faith *(pistis*) is not, simply, propositional belief. That could and does ebb and flow. In a word, that becomes another as the context demands, the faith that the fanatic wants but does not want is trust.

The earnestness, the self-concern, that yearns for God and nothing less, is also a concern for truth. The springs of faith are also a font of doubt.[30] For better or worse, Kierkegaard's great souled man is wedded to the idea and so the objective worry takes another hand-wringing form. The nagging concern is no longer a question of the idea's credibility, it is, instead, a question that the questioning individual is careful to include himself in. The ethical announces itself in pangs of conscience, in a feeling that one has fallen too far short and so is not ethical. One of faith's many telling words is an echo of the same; faith announces itself as a feeling that one has fallen too far short and so is without faith:

> The relationship to Christ is this—a person tests for himself whether Christ is everything to him, and then says, I put everything into this. But I cannot get an immediate certainty about my relationship to Christ. I cannot get an immediate certainty about whether I have faith, for to have faith is this very dialectical suspension which is continually in fear and trembling and yet never despairs; faith is precisely this infinite worry about oneself *(Selvbekymring)* which keeps one awake in risking everything, this worry about oneself *(Selvbekymring)* as to whether one really has faith—and behold it is precisely this worry about oneself *(Selvbekymring)* that is faith.[31]

38   Gordon Marino: *Kierkegaard in the Present Age*

The fanatic cannot understand such desperate thoughts. After all, he knows where he will sit, if not at the right, then on the left hand of the Father. As Vigilius Haufniensis describes him:

> He knows it all... He talks of meeting before the throne of God and knows how many times one should bow. He knows everything, like the man who can prove a mathematical proposition when the letters are ABC, but not when the letters are DEF.[32]

Where interest goes, consciousness follows. Inasmuch as the zealot's passion is poured out, he is unselfconscious. Unselfconscious as he is, faith is not a question of his relation to God, but rather of God's relation to dogma. Even if the religious maniac sees himself as God's personal envoy, it is all in a quasi-formalistic setting, as a skewed sort of objective fact. No matter what the fanatic thinks he believes, his God is an impersonal, objectified deity. The passion that might have given rise to an awareness of himself and God as subject serves only to infuse his object world with an unusual intensity.

NOTES

[1] Unless otherwise stated, textual references are to Søren Kierkegaard's *Concluding Unscientific Postscript*, trans. and ed. Howard and Edna Hong (Princeton: Princeton University Press, 1992). Each reference to the English translation is followed by the corresponding volume and page(s) from the Collected Works (Søren Kierkegaard *Samlede Værker*), ed. A.B. Drachmann, J.L. Heiberg and H.O. Lange, Vols. I-XX, in the 3rd edition (Copenhagen: Gyldendal). Also, following the 3rd edition reference is the 1st edition reference in parentheses.

[2] It is critical to note that S.K. does not dispense with this criterion when he defines the truth as subjectivity. Consider for example pp. 191-192, IX 157 (VII 159); 197, IX 164 (VII 164-165).

[3] 150, IX 124 (VII 123-124); 189, IX 157-158 (VII 157).

[4] 203, IX 169 (VII 169).

[5] 201, IX 167-168 (VII 168).

[6] 194, IX 162 (VII 162).

[7] 194n, IX 162n (VII 162n).

[8] 301, IX 9 (VII 258); 348, IX 49 (VII 302).

⁹ *Philosophical Fragments or a Fragment of Philosophy*, originally translated and edited by David F. Swenson, new introduction and commentary by Niels Thulstrup, translation revised and commentary translated by Howard and Edna Hong (Princeton: Princeton University Press, 1985), 106f, VI 68f (IV 268f).

¹⁰ "If a man occupied himself, all his life through, solely with logic, he would nevertheless not become logic; he must therefore himself exist in different categories" (93, IX 80 (VII 73)).

¹¹ 37, IX 36 (VII 26).

¹² See Søren Kierkegaard, *Johannes Climacus* (in the same volume as *Philosophical Fragments* or, *De Omnibus Dubitandum Est*, trans. and ed. Howard and Edna Hong (Princeton: Princeton University Press), 167f; *Papirer*, ed. P.A. Heiberg, V. Kuhr, E. Torsting, N. Thulstrup (Copenhagen: Gyldendal, 1968-70), Vol. IV, B 1, pp. 145f. For a valuable commentary on Kierkegaard's conception of consciousness see John Elrod's *Being and Existence in Kierkegaard's Pseudonymous Works* (Princeton, NJ: Princeton University Press, 1975), 43-53.

¹³ 23, IX 23 (VII 12).

¹⁴ 27, IX 27 (VII 16).

¹⁵ 27, IX 27 (VII 16).

¹⁶ 167, IX 139 (VII 138-139).

¹⁷ 31, IX 31 (VII 20).

¹⁸ 31n, IX 31 (VII 20n).

¹⁹ 35, XI 34 (VII 24); also see Niels Thulstrup's *Commentary on Kierkegaard's Concluding Unscientific Postscript*, trans. Robert J. Widenmann (Princeton, NJ: Princeton University Press, 1984), 174.

²⁰ 507, X 184 (VII 441).

²¹ No one, not even Kierkegaard himself, could give more gripping expression to the idea that faith is a collision with the understanding than Dostoevsky has in a missive to a scarcely known benefactor. Mme. Fonsivin is in bad spirits. Dostoevsky tries to console her. Look to the last of these lines written in exile:

> I want to say to you, about myself, that I am a child of this age, a child of unfaith and scepticism and probably (indeed I know it) should remain so to the end of my life. How dreadfully has it tormented me (and torments me even now), this longing for faith, which is all the stronger for the proofs I have against it. And yet God gives me sometimes the moments of perfect peace; in such moments I love and believe that I am loved; in such moments I have formulated my creed, wherein all is clear and holy to me. This creed is extremely

simple; here it is: I believe that there is nothing lovelier, deeper, more sympathetic, more rational, more manly, and more perfect than the Savior: I say to myself with jealous love that not only is there no one else like Him, but that there could be no one. I would even say more: If anyone could prove to me that Christ is outside the truth, and if the truth really did exclude Christ, I should prefer to stay with Christ and not with truth (March, 1854).

Also see Kresten Nordentoft's *Kierkegaard's Psychology* (Pittsburgh: Duquesne University Press, 1972), 138-142.

[22] Sigmund Freud, *Civilization and its Discontents* (1930), standard edition, Vol. XXI (London: Hogarth Press, 1957), 74. See also 84-85.

[23] Louis Pojman works this question into a critique of Climacus' conception of faith. See his The *Logic of Subjectivity, Kierkegaard's Philosophy of Religion* (University of Alabama: The University of Alabama Press, 1984), 103-117.

[24] 30, IX 30 (VII 19); 32-34, IX 31-33 (VII 21-23).

[25] 129, IX 107 (VII 105).

[26] Some of Kierkegaard's misguiding commentators have been taken in by Climacus who often writes as though the object of religious conviction were a matter of relative, if not absolute, indifference, e.g., 13, IX 108 (VII 4-5); 199, IX 166-167 (VII 166-167). The textual evidence is both abundant and plain—that Climacus' creator did not hold this spiritually perilous position.

[27] 203, IX 170 (VII 170); 210, IX 175 (VII 176).

[28] See Alastair Hannay's *Kierkegaard* (Boston: Routledge & Kegan Paul, 1982), 97-122.

[29] Mind you, however, it is not as though the devout go without any sign of having found the way. Quite the contrary, Climacus, and most especially Kierkegaard, repeatedly insist—leap and you shall find, faith brings its own proof (26, IX 27 (VII 15-16); 174, IX 145 (VII 144-145); also see *Papirer*, X, I, Z 481, p. 30). It goes without saying that this fact cannot be applied as a spiritual formula. That is, faith will not come to the calculating individual who figures that by believing he can conjure up the proof his belief cannot do without. As though belief could ever get started under these conditions! As though the figure of Christ were an exotic species of working hypotheses! Once more, Kierkegaard points to a certain kind of certitude that comes with commitment, but the peace and quiet confidence that accompanies this act of trust needs to be distin-

guished from the cocksurity of fanaticism and less passionate forms
of objectivity.

30 Søren Kierkegaard, *Johannes Climacus* (in the same volume as
    Philosophical Fragments), 166f (IV, B 1, 144f). *Johannes Climacus* is
    also known as *De Omnibus Dubitandum Est.*

31 *Søren Kierkegaard's Journals and Papers*, ed. and trans. Howard and
    Edna Hong, assisted by Gregor Malantschuk (Bloomington: Indi-
    ana University Press, 1967), 1:108 entry 255 N.B. (IX A 32 n.d.,
    1848) (This is a slightly amended version of the Hongs' translation.).

32 Kierkegaard, *Concept of Anxiety* 139-140 (IV 406-407).

CHAPTER 3

THE PLACE OF REASON
IN KIERKEGAARD'S ETHICS

Alasdair MacIntyre's *After Virtue* stands as one of the most important works in moral philosophy to be published in the second half of the twentieth century. In this text, MacIntyre assumes the bankruptcy of the meta-ethical project of grounding ethics in neutral reason. He bids us to return once again to the Aristotelian position of placing the concept of virtue at the core of our reflections on ethics. MacIntyre has, in effect, single handedly resurrected virtue ethics. As we will see, Kierkegaard has a protagonist's role in MacIntyre's history of western ethics. In this chapter, we will examine and assess MacIntyre's reading of Kierkegaard.

What role, if any, does Kierkegaard assign to reason in ethics? Making constant reference to a book that challenges Kierkegaard's account of the ethical (Alasdair MacIntyre's *After Virtue*) the essay that follows is a reply to this question. Through some fault of his own, Kierkegaard has left MacIntyre and others with the impression that he did not believe the choice to live in ethical terms could be defended on rational grounds. *Contra* MacIntyre, I shall argue that Kierkegaard does in fact offer reasons for advancing from the first to the second stage on life's way. However, having defended Kierkegaard from one charge of irrationalism, I argue that when considered as a moral phenomenologist Kierkegaard did in fact underestimate the role of reason. Thus MacIntyre is right to complain that Kierkegaard paid insufficient attention to the problem of adjudicating between conflicting moral claims.

I. A synopsis of MacIntyre's reading

MacIntyre hypothesizes that in the late 17th and early 18th centuries, morality emerged as a concept without a home, either in theology, law, or aesthetics.[1] Unhoused as he claims it was, the need for a justification of morality loomed up in the "enlightenment project." This project first failed, and with all hope being abandoned in the coming of a messianic justification, the more decisive cultural event took place—the project was perceived as a failure. It is in the protracted here and now of this dispiriting perception that MacIntyre situates the present dark age, an age which envisages moral debate in terms of a confrontation between incompatible and incommensurable moral premises and moral commitment as the expression of a criterionless choice between such premises, a type of choice for which no rational justification can be given.[2]

Once again, Kierkegaard plays a key role in this, the first of MacIntyre's multi-volume philosophical drama, or at least the Kierkegaard of *Either/Or* does for it is with this text that MacIntyre identifies Kierkegaard. Apart from one glancing reference, no other works are touched upon, let alone treated. MacIntyre isolates three key features of *Either/Or*. For one, he notes that the book's mode of presentation and content are mirror images of one another.[3] As for the content, MacIntyre insists that through all the voices in *Either/Or* one message is bell-clear, there are no rational grounds for choosing between the ethical and the esthetic.[4] There are no real arguments, only hurrahs and gestures of commendation. And so, MacIntyre glosses, we find in this work the perfect coincidence of form and content. Once more, the thesis is that there are nothing but commendations, and commendations are all the reader gets. 'A' commends the life of the esthete, 'B' (Judge Wilhelm) commends the life of duty, and the editor, Victor Emerita, arbitrarily arranges the recommendations of 'A' and 'B.'

Feature number two is this—for Kierkegaard, and not coincidentally, for Kant, "the ethical is presented as that realm in which principles have authority over us independently of our attitudes, preferences and feelings."[5] But whence comes this absolute authority? For MacIntyre? For MacIntyre's Kierkegaard? And finally for Kierkegaard? To query number one MacIntyre replies:

> To answer this question (whence comes the authority of ethical principles) consider what kind of authority any principle has which it is open to choose to regard as authoritative.[6]

Be it a principle of practical reasoning or the eleventh commandment, said principle or commandment has as much authority as I can give reasons for heeding it, so that "a principle for the choice of which no reasons could be given would be a principle devoid of authority."[7] On MacIntyre's reading, Kierkegaard offers no reasons for choosing the ethical over the esthetic and so he presents Kierkegaard as blundering—the ethical has absolute authority, the ethical has no authority.[8]

Finally, MacIntyre calls attention to what he takes to be the fact that *Either/Or* is a highly conservative document, and he adds that the book's hidebound quality is at odds with the novel form of moral self-justification that Kierkegaard is depicted as peddling. True, it could be argued that the author of *Either/Or* was very soon to become, if he wasn't already, a spiritual insurgent of the first order, but just the same, MacIntyre persists in claiming that the Kierkegaard of 1842 was trying to scribble in a "new practical underpinning for an older and inherited way of life."[9] MacIntyre continues, "It is perhaps this combination of novelty and tradition which accounts for the incoherence at the heart of Kierkegaard's position."[10]

2. WHO IS MACINTYRE'S KIERKEGAARD?

Anyone who has browsed through, much less written an introduction or two on Kierkegaard knows well enough that if you must equate Kierkegaard with the author of *Either/Or,* do so with trepidation, for more than any of his many pseudonymous works, Kierkegaard held this, his bestseller, at a distinct arm's length. MacIntyre has been the full length of the corpus, and he has written a pair of critical summaries, but he still draws the equation with insufficient reluctance. To be sure, the reader is officially informed that one could argue what many scholars feel free to assume, namely, that if there is an ethical theory in *Either/Or*, Kierkegaard himself did not hold it. MacIntyre acknowledges that even if Kierkegaard did take the position *After Virtue* nails him to, it was not for long. Though he does not indicate how he thinks Kierkegaard's ethics might have changed, the author is careful to whisper that by 1845 and with the publication of *Philosophical Fragments*, Kierkegaard's characterization of the ethical "has changed radically." [11] But note well, this radical change was abundantly clear as early as 1843 in *Frygt og Bæven*[12] that is, less than a year after completing *Either/Or*.[13] This much of a confession can be dragged out of *After Virtue*—if MacIntyre's Kierkegaard was Kierkegaard at all, it was only for a few of Kierkegaard's earliest semesters.

If, as the narrative insists, the Kierkegaard of *Either/Or* is laboring to lay a foundation for morals, then it would be absurd to identify him with any of his esthetic alter-egos. But more than trying to ground morals, it is critical to this chapter of MacIntyre's history that Kierkegaard be considered a regular bastion of conservatism. Kierkegaard is supposed to be confused and incoherent, and the source of his muddled state is supposed to be the implacable need to combine immiscibles—radical choice and conservative values.[14] In point of fact, MacIntyre hints at what he is about to do, namely, to fuse the figure of Kierkegaard with that of the conservative and orotund Judge Wilhelm (or 'B'). Here are the fingerprints; while Kierkegaard is nowhere and everywhere in *Either/Or*. "perhaps we detect his presence most of all in the belief that he puts into the mouth of 'B'..."[15] There can be no doubt about it, so far as MacIntyre is concerned, Kierkegaard's moral theory is the latent content behind the Judge's manifest moralizing. For, if not the Judge, then who is the credulous curator of traditional values that MacIntyre has as his Kierkegaard of 1842? Note, however, that the Judge's style, his spoony Christianity, to say nothing of his self-contradictions are signs enough that this frequently touching, but often boorish pate is hardly a man after Kierkegaard's own heart.[16]

But are the ethics of Judge Wilhelm the ethics of the young Kierkegaard? Though I am by no means certain,[17] I move to accept MacIntyre's donee, for who, after all, can argue with someone as close to Kierkegaard as Kierkegaard's Johannes Climacus? And as Johannes tells it, the second part (of the *Concluding Unscientific Postscript*) represents "an ethical individuality existing on the basis of the ethical."[18] The equation drawn and accepted, let us examine MacIntyre's claim that in *Either/Or* Kierkegaard is not only representing the ethical but announcing the utter irrationality of it. According to this announcement, no one person can give another reason for understanding his or her life in ethical terms. No, as MacIntyre reads it, the choice of moral striving and guilt is a criterionless choice. But does MacIntyre's description fit?

3. The so-called criterionless-choice

Although he will disregard Kierkegaard's self-explanations a page later, MacIntyre is right to report that "Kierkegaard's professed intention in designing the pseudonyms of *Enten/Eller* was to present the reader with an ultimate choice", *enten*—the ethical, *eller*—the esthetic mode of living and regarding life. Hypothesizing again, MacIntyre suggests, "suppose that someone confronts the choice between them, as yet having embraced neither."[19] Well then, that someone is a self-deluded esthete. For Kierkegaard, there is no sitting on the fence between selves. If you have not chosen, you are an esthete, but if you are really facing the choice, you have already chosen to choose.

There simply is no earnestly facing the choice qua an individual who has yet to choose, for to acknowledge the choice is to affirm that you have a self, which marks the second, not the first, stage on life's way. And that in one breath is why Kierkegaard believed he only needed "to present the reader with an ultimate choice."[20]

MacIntyre obliquely discloses the impossibility of the Kierkegaardian self on the fence. He comments that for Kierkegaard and certainly Judge Wilhelm, there is no choosing the esthetic.[21] MacIntyre writes as though he believed the infallibility of the first genuine choice follows from the passion with which it is made—and that is that. It isn't. Of course, once the inwardness, which earmarks the ethical is present, the choice is made; and so again, one cannot earnestly hover between life A and life B. But even apart from this, there is no choosing the esthetic, simply because there is no one to choose it. As our public servant defines it, "the esthetical in a person is that by which he is spontaneously and immediately what he is" ("det æsthetiske i et Menneske er det, hvorved han umiddelbar er det, han er"[22]). Be he or she a sensualist, sincere social activist, or knight of faith, everyone has, or is, their esthetic side, and Kierkegaard repeatedly warns that we had better remember it. Once more, the earnest choice of oblivion that MacIntyre reproaches Kierkegaard for overlooking would amount to an earnest choice not to choose. But the choice not to choose would be the very kind of serious choice that the purely esthetic precludes. Rightly or wrongly, the Kierkegaard that MacIntyre's narrative takes to task has it that there is no leaping in and out of the lethe of immediacy. There is despair and defiance, but no dashing the brains out of self-consciousness.[23] The individual who is either gullible or serious enough to come to the uncoerced conclusion that he must choose between one self-perspective and another, is, by Kierkegaard's standards, a pretty serious fellow who has, in his very quandary, already acknowledged his ethical identity.

All unacceptable hypotheses aside, MacIntyre explains that the self, so situated between selves, could not be given reasons for the final imperative: I should choose the ethical, or for that matter, I should choose the esthetic.[24] Echoing *After Virtue's* analysis, the esthetic is no choice at all and so for the purposes of the reconstructed argument we may proceed—any chain of moral reasons that might be stretched before an esthete presupposes his regarding those reasons as having force. Choose good and evil, the moralist imagines he is arguing, for by relating to yourself in those terms you will best, "serve the demands of duty, for to live in that way will be to accept moral perfection as a good and so give a certain kind of meaning to one's actions."[25] But what does a Sybarite care about duty, moral perfection, or meaning? Nothing, answers MacIntyre in his synopsis; for Kierkegaard it is only by radical choice, that is, a choice for which no reasons can be adduced that we come into the ethical, and it is only by radical choice that the ethical comes into its foundations.

Judging both from his encyclopedia entry[26] and *After Virtue*, MacIntyre has been pressing long and hard to inoculate every student against what he takes to be the dangerous charms of Kierkegaard's irrationalism. The already mentioned scourge term is the so-called "criterionless choice" that MacIntyre's Kierkegaard enjoins us to make. And what renders the choice of the ethical a criterionless choice? Once again, the fact that it is supposed to be a choice of first principles renders it a criterionless choice. And if the proof is in the act of choice? It makes no difference. If a converted Don Juan cannot provide the next Don Juan with compelling reasons to follow his lead, his conversion is without a basis in reason. And what is to count as a compelling reason? As I understand MacIntyre, so long as the esthete has a choice that reason cannot mindlessly make, say the choice whether or not to give force to appeals to a meaningful life, he has no reason. But, to cover the same ground again, we always have a choice, which is not to say that we always have a coin to toss. There is, as the sequel to *After Virtue* concedes,[27] something in between chance and demonstration; or more to my point, from the fact that one life view cannot be strictly deduced from a crumbling or absent other, it does not follow that the choice of the one, from within the context of the other, is necessarily arbitrary.[28] Besides, the Judge explains that and why it is in an individual's enlightened self-interest to choose the ethical.

Make no mistake about it, A and B are not from different planets. Whether or not it is to his ultimate discredit, if the Judge could step out of his pages, he would be quick to remind MacIntyre that there is more continuity (equilibrium) between the ethical and the esthetic than MacIntyre encourages us to imagine. Even assuming that the Judge has made the turn he is prodding A to make, he has not left the esthetic behind.[29] He need not march back and forth to the Royal Library and lucubrate for months on end in order to reconstruct the world as seen through the categories of hedonic interests. The Judge argues that A has every good reason, every rational motive, for choosing to live seriously as opposed to indifferently. There is only space and call for a sample of these briefs,[30] but each comes to this—an ethical existence is superior to and/or a cure for the ills endemic to estheticism.

No more an ethical theorist than an ethical rigorist, the Judge charges that there is no unity in a life that cannot sit still.[31] Since there is no unity in his life, A cannot provide a coherent account of himself.[32] And in the event A couldn't care less about giving a coherent account of his life, B admonishes, "he who cannot reveal himself cannot love, and he who cannot love is the most unhappy man of all."[33] Everyone wants to be happy, therefore one should choose the ethical, for it is only by that act of choice that a person can create the ballast that makes unity and happiness possible. In 1839 Kierkegaard remarked, "longing is the umbilical cord of the higher life." The Judge more than agrees,[34] he fills in the content of what he takes these ubiquitous longings to be. There are, he assumes, universal desires for *inter alia* a life view, meaning, serenity, and as mentioned, happiness. In short, the allegedly debunking question of the esthete's "giving force" to the terms of the Judge's appeals does not arise. True, every desire will appear differently according to the categories through which it is conceived, but both the Judge and Kierkegaard suppose that there is enough continuity to reason the esthete out of one conception and toward another. And so B writes as though to grant "think of these ends as you may, there is more meaning, peace of mind, and happiness in a life devoted to duty than in one devoted to fleeing boredom." And if beauty be your lodestar then take heed, there is more beauty to be garnered with an eye fixed upon the Good than with one trained for the interesting.[35]

Finally both character and creator assume that despair is everyone's negative Prime Mover. On solid evidence, if not confession, the Judge diagnoses his friend as a case of intense (and so for Kierkegaard, promising) despair. Though only possessing a balm, B offers the remedy that Kierkegaard's anthropology has A groping for. What is twice as important, he argues, and with Kierkegaard's blessings, that where the esthete has a goal—e.g., happiness, success—the conditions for satisfaction are always beyond the ken of his control.[36] This, having one's axis outside of oneself, emerges as the definition for despair and from it B draws out the conclusion that a fleeting, unduty-bound existence is necessarily a despairing one.[37] Despite the curtain of problems that Johannes de Silentio is poised to let drop, the Judge assures his distraught companion that nothing can come between an individual and his duty. So again, if only by reason of its being a cure, A should choose the ethical and by implication, he should choose to regard himself as the culprit responsible for his despair.[38]

Even Aristotle throws up his hands here and there. There is, for instance, no reasoning with the underground man who refuses to accept happiness as his final good. If the choice that Kierkegaard worked into his every work were an unloaded one between box A and box B, MacIntyre would have his point—but it isn't.[39] Explaining their inevitable failure to make compelling moral sense, MacIntyre remarks that Diderot, Smith, and alas, Kierkegaard, "all reject any teleological view of human nature, and of man as having an essence which defines his true end." And this is "why their project of finding a basis for morality had to fail."[40] I cannot vouch for the other defendants, but the author behind the editor of *Either/Or* has his *telos*, and it is relative to it that choice finds its rational grounds. Whether or not Kierkegaard has the right telos remains another gaping question, but the telos is assumed to be there, pushing from behind (despair) and pulling from above (longing). All children of miraculous faith aside, every person is naturally in despair, some much more intensely than others. Some much more intensely than others, everyone naturally yearns to be free of the despair which Kierkegaard contends we are all individually spinning. Aristotle's *Ethics* presupposes his psychology, and likewise Kierkegaard's concept of choice presupposes a universal but not universally recognized need to be whole. Despair is sin, sin the universal sickness, and faith alone the cure, which can only begin to be secured by a choice that A has yet to make and other choices that B (the Judge) may need his C and D to awaken him to.

4. A CRITICAL NOTE

Understandably, Kierkegaard scholars complain that Kierkegaard was simply not trying to do the kinds of things that MacIntyre chides him for failing to do. As *After Virtue* tells it, Kierkegaard perceived Kant's failure to provide a basis for morals, panicked, and took up the search for the next Holy Grail. Now, there are entries aplenty on Kant in the *Papirer*, and it is true that Kierkegaard recognized that Kant had not proven the esthetic life to be one of self-contradiction.[41] Nevertheless, there are no textual signs that this recognition ever prodded Kierkegaard into taking up the foundational project that MacIntyre charges him with bungling. Kierkegaard wrote and wrote about his writing and there is no hint of his aspiring to produce a basis for morals, and of this MacIntyre is well aware. Why then the decision to ignore Kierkegaard's hyperconscious intentions? Does MacIntyre believe that while Kierkegaard thought he was writing about choice in fundamental connection with the formation of the self and the purification of the will, he was actually struggling to solve a problem that he was unaware of being driven by? Is there a latent appeal to the unconscious behind MacIntyre's manifest historicizing? There has to be.

I have no innate aversion to the idea that neither Kierkegaard nor MacIntyre necessarily knows what he is really up to; just the same, I see no reason for automatically dismissing an author's long-held and continuously-stated intentions. MacIntyre has a lot of territory to cover and naturally travels in seven league boots, oblivious to the nitpickers. But is it nitpicking to complain that MacIntyre has not shown Kierkegaard's self-explanations to be inadequate? He has not justified his appeal to oblique purposes by showing us why he takes Kierkegaard to be in the dark about his projects. If I am any judge of the present age, someone is bound to reply that the story is the demonstration, but that is a rather unconvincing story. As some of Freud's early case studies will attest, the richness of a narrative is no proof of the details of that narrative. Far from it, historical narratives that roll smoothly and comprehensively along usually do so because they plow every-thing under. And for all his epiphanies, it must be said that MacIntyre has done his share of plowing. But now for one of the epiphanies.

5. The place of reason in the moral life

Though we may not have access to the justifications, Kierkegaard certainly held that there are universal moral truths. There is, however, another critical message in the bottle of *After Virtue*, and I shall argue that this message sticks. As I read him, MacIntyre charges that Kierkegaard fails to acknowledge the role of reason in the moral life, and in a related blindspot, he fails to appreciate, let alone help us come to grips with, a fact that unsettles many a conscience and nearly every ethical theorist—the fact of moral diversity.

Kierkegaard's greatest service may well have been to paint the ideal or at least one constellation of ideals from the inside out. A psychological realist in his own right, Kierkegaard teaches us to see with discernment just what the world looks like through ideals otherwise quite easily bandied about. Nevertheless, for all of the arresting detail of his portraits of perfectly fallen creatures striving to live in their thoughts of the right and the good, there is something missing. As MacIntyre observes, Kierkegaard pictures the earnest life as though there were nothing to it but what we moderns and post-moderns might call commitment. In his words and silences, Kierkegaard affirms that behind every piece of moral confusion there is a will flapping in the breeze of whims. If you don't rightly know what to do, then you don't really will to do what is right.

That moral worth has as little to do with moral reasoning as it does with knowledge, is indirectly revealed in Kierkegaard's jottings on the method of indirect communication. In his outlined but never delivered lectures on the ethico-religious dialectic of communication, Kierkegaard teaches that in the realm of the truly important there is much for a moral teacher to do, but nothing to teach; there is no object of communication, no knowledge to be conveyed. Kierkegaard's thinking is clear and Kantian enough. Moral duties are universal. If, however, I was wanting in knowledge, then I wouldn't be possessed of the duties that my sense of guilt assures me obtain. And Kierkegaard avows that if there is one thing I can trust it is my sense of guilt. Thus, while I may require a moral teacher to prevent me from obscuring

the knowledge to which my duty and guilt bear witness, I do not
need anyone to put me in the know.

As everyone knows, Kierkegaard believed his age to be suffering
from an excess of mental activity; but in the excess of his struggles
against such excesses, Kierkegaard could easily lead one to believe
that every act of deliberation is an ethical evasion, that is, the will
using reason to confuse and so excuse itself from what it now
knows and is now trying to forget is its unconditional duty.[42] A
grand master of suspicion, Kierkegaard was right to observe that
reason often functions in the service of the pleasure/complacency
principle, but is the abuse of reason a good reason to sow blanket
suspicions about reason? My reason says, "No."

As I have complained, MacIntyre is mistaken to think that
Kierkegaard does not offer reasons for choosing the ethical, but
the justification of particular ethical precepts is altogether another matter. To reiterate, MacIntyre argues that a principle has
as much authority as we have reasons for abiding by that principle.
As MacIntyre notes, Kierkegaard could not disagree more. An
enemy of every form of meliorism, Kierkegaard is unambiguous,
the ethical no less than the religious is "the unconditionally
unconditional." Just as unambiguously, Kierkegaard warns that
while the unconditional has its reasons, the provision of those
reasons relativizes it and thus subtracts rather than increases
authority.[43] MacIntyre reports that Kierkegaard was the first to
sever the connection between reason and authority.[44] Again,
Kierkegaard couldn't disagree more. According to his chronology
of emerging ideas, it was only in the age of pure reason that people
began to require explanations of their imperatives, Either way,
MacIntyre is on the mark, for Kierkegaard the force of our oughts
does not rest upon the answers to our why questions.

Kierkegaard all but takes it as a given that we ought to do what
our father, worldly and other-worldly, commands us to do. The
ideal is obedience, and for all its other merits, obedience is not an
ideal that is likely to prod consciousness-raising about either the
interests of others or the consequences of our actions. But why
should it? These are precisely the kinds of conditions that
devotion to the unconditional has to be careful to blinker itself to.
Though this is not to advise that one should ruminate until the

moment to act has passed, it is irresponsible to cut the process of reflection short with the reflection that a choice must eventually be made, and besides, so long as you can imagine that you possess the best intentions, you cannot go morally wrong. But what is more important, doing the right thing or having the right intention? For Kierkegaard, as much as for Schopenhauer,[45] it is the intention, the relative purity of heart[46] that determines the moral worth of an action. The rest is external, which for Kierkegaard is again to say, accidental and unimportant. Take this page from the Journal, a page which happens to find its way into the papers of Victor Eremita:

> The main point is still that one should not be diverted by the external. When, in order to subvert the position that there is an absolute in morality, an appeal is made to variations in custom and use and such shocking examples as savages putting their parents to death, attention is centered merely upon the external. That is to say, if it could be proved that savages maintain that a person ought to hate his parents, it would be quite another matter; but this is not their thought; they believe that one should love them, and the error is only in the way of expressing it. For it is clear that the savages do not intend to harm their parents but to do good to them.[47]

Note the initial intimation—such questions are not raised in good faith, but rather in an attempt to subvert and so to excuse oneself from the unconditionality of absolutes. Slit your parent's throats or sacrifice your life taking care of them, it is all essentially the same, so long as your intentions are good. For the one who finally gave us the esthetic of morals that Kant lacked the Muse to write, the main task is not to allow externals—i.e., the perceived consequences of our actions—to make us flinch. As though perceived consequences had nothing whatsoever to do with our intentions.

The inordinate prominence that Kierkegaard gives to our intentions has its natural shadow in a delusory de-emphasis on the question of what precisely is to be done. This imbalance is nowhere more apparent than in the lack of urgency Kierkegaard shows with respect to questions of social justice. And yet, it hardly needs to be written that our virtuoso of inwardness did not decry all forms of reflection. While Kierkegaard did not trouble himself unduly about the moral worth of this action as opposed to that, his conscience was downright yeasty when it came to trying to decide whether or not it was God's will that he do X or Y. Make no bones about it, he was quite concrete on this score, or as Kant would have judged him—he was quite fantastic. For Kierkegaard, believing in a personal God entails the belief that God may at any time be personally involved in the events of this world. Thus, the true believer utters his intercessory and petitionary prayers; and thus, Kierkegaard rather quietly insists that the knight of faith is ever searching the palimpsestal text of daily events for a directive "hint from God."[48]

Kierkegaard was not much concerned with trying to hammer out the right secular "oughts," and in MacIntyre's terms, MacIntyre is essentially correct—for Kierkegaard "there were no great problems of interpretation," or at least not beyond deciding whether or not he was an exception to duties otherwise accepted. But when it came to discerning what it meant to believe in God, Kierkegaard's reflections render it easy to see how Kierkegaard came to associate reflection with dizziness. For this essay's final illustration, in a much abused teaching, Jesus tells us that the poor will always be with us.[49] He also commands us to be merciful. Yet how can a peasant with neither money nor power be merciful? Kierkegaard understood well that the impecunious have plenty to wrestle with, but he was in his own way generous enough to add this characteristically Kierkegaardian scruple. The poor ought to be merciful enough not to make the filthy rich feel filthy about their riches:

> So, then, the discourse addresses itself to you, you wretched one who are able to do nothing at all: Do not forget to be merciful! This comfort, that you are able to be merciful, to say nothing of the comfort that you are merciful, is far greater than if I were able to assure you that the most powerful will show you mercifulness. Be merciful to us more fortunate ones! Your care-filled life is like a dangerous protest against the loving Governance; therefore you have it in your power to alarm the rest of us—so be merciful! Truly, how much mercifulness is shown toward the powerful and fortunate by such an unfortunate! Indeed, which is more merciful: powerfully to remedy

the needs of others or quietly to suffer and patiently to watch
mercifully lest one disturb the joy and happiness of others?[50]

The answer worked out with both rigor and consistency is that
the one fortunate in his misfortune is the more merciful, but I
present this only as an instance of the kinds of interpretive problems that Kierkegaard recognized and of the kind of reflection
he would seem to recommend. There are double, triple, and
quadruple reflections upon his duties to God, but very little scru-
pling about his duties to his fellow human beings.

Unfortunately, MacIntyre pays no heed to Kierkegaard's rather
congenial critique of the tradition MacIntyre is trying to resuscitate, but as one distinctively Lutheran line of that critique repeats,
the opposite of sin is not virtue, but faith.[51] Whether it be for the
reasons Kierkegaard himself adduced, or for those woven into
After Virtue, Kierkegaard had no faith that reason could compel
us to compel ourselves to make the sacrifices that Kierkegaard
understood to be the signature of the ethical. The conquest of
self-love, to say nothing of the demon Kant could not discern,
defiance, requires a much stricter taskmaster than we can bring to
bear upon ourselves. To put it in words that some claim have seen
their day and their twilight, it is only by the love/fear of God that
we are able to slip out of the snare of self-love and willfulness, and
that—getting outside of oneself—is what distinguishes the
ethico-religious from the esthetic. On this decisive point,
MacIntyre's reading of Kierkegaard is true to the author that I
know; for Kierkegaard of early, middle, and late, moral reasoning
and ethical theorizing have as little to do with being moral as they
have to do with the quest which Kierkegaard marks as singularly
important—the quest for a pure will.

NOTES

[1] Alasdair MacIntyre, *After Virtue: A Study in Moral Theory*, 2nd edition,
    (Notre Dame: University of Notre Dame Press, 1984).
[2] Ibid., p. 39.
[3] Ibid., p. 39.
[4] Ibid., p. 40f.
[5] Ibid., p. 41.
[6] Ibid., p. 42.

[7] Ibid., p. 42.

[8] Ibid., p. 42.

[9] Ibid., p. 43.

[10] Ibid. p. 43.

[11] Ibid., p. 41.

[12] It is clear that MacIntyre recognizes *Fear and Trembling* for the counterexample to his reading that it is. As MacIntyre's history repeats, Kierkegaard discovered the concept of radical choice and put it to the task of forming a basis for morals (AV 33). But if anyone ever made a radical choice it was Abraham, and he was anything but ethically justified. Just the opposite, as Johannes de Silentio puts it, no matter what the religious expression might be, "The ethical expression for what Abraham did is that he meant to murder Isaac" (Søren Kierkegaard, *Fear and Trembling*, ed. and trans. Howard and Edna Hong (Princeton: Princeton University Press, 1983), 30 (III 82) (Note: following every Hong edition page reference is the page reference of the quote or section from the Danish 1st edition or the Papirer).

[13] By the latest reckoning we are actually talking about a period of approximately six months. See Alastair Hannay's and Niels Jørgen Cappelørn's "The Period of Composition of Kierkegaard's Published Works," *Kierkegaardiana* 9 (1974): 132-146.

[14] MacIntyre, *op. cit.,* p. 43.

[15] Ibid., p. 41.

[16] For an excellent likeness of the Judge see Stephen Dunning's *Kierkegaard's Dialectic of Inwardness* (Princeton: Princeton University Press, 1985), 75ff.

[17] In his *Kierkegaard* (Routledge: London, 1982) Alastair Hannay meticulously shows that one need not go beyond the covers of *Either/Or* to find a critique of the Judge's 'both/and' view that one has only to will the conventional (*'Det Almene'*) and all will be reconciled-inner and outer, spirit and flesh, ethical and aesthetic. See pp. 58-63.

[18] Søren Kierkegaard, *Concluding Unscientific Postscript*, trans. Howard and Edna Hong (Princeton: Princeton University Press, 1992), 253 (VII 214).

[19] MacIntyre, *op. cit.,* p. 40.

[20] Ibid., p. 40.

[21] Ibid., p. 40-41. I follow George Stack here. See his "Kierkegaard's Analysis of Choice: The Aristotelian Model," *The Personalist* 52 (1971): 643-661.

[22] Søren Kierkegaard, *Either/Or, Volume II*, trans. Howard and Edna Hong. (Princeton: Princeton University Press, 1987), 178 (II 161).

[23] This is certainly one of the central claims of Kierkegaard's *Sickness Unto Death.*

[24] MacIntyre., *op. cit.*, p. 40.

[25] Ibid., p. 40.

[26] *The Encyclopedia of Philosophy*, ed. Paul Edwards, 4 vols., (New York: Macmillan Press, 1967), 4:336-340; see also MacIntyre's *A Short History of Ethics* (New York: Macmillan Press, 1966), 215-218.

[27] MacIntyre, *Whose Justice? Which Rationality?* (Indiana: Notre Dame Press, 1988).

[28] And so I would argue that the author of *After Virtue* is working with a somewhat hyperbolic notion of what is to count for a moral justification. For authors who have come to a conclusion similar to my own, see C. Stephen Evans' "Where there is a will there's a way: Kierkegaard's theory of action" in *Writing the Politics of Difference*, ed. H.J. Silverman (Albany: SUNY Press, 1991) 73-88; see also Anthony Rudd's *Kierkegaard and the Limits of the Ethical* (New York: Oxford University Press, 1993).

[29] Kierkegaard, *Either/Or* II:177-178 (II 161-162).

[30] For more exhaustive presentations of the Judge's defense of the ethical, see Harold Ofstad's "Morality, Choice, and Inwardness: Judge Wilhelm's distinction between the esthetic and the ethical way of life," *Inquiry*, 1965, 8:33-73.

[31] Kierkegaard, *Either/Or* II:248 (II 223), 262ff (II 235ff).

[32] Kierkegaard, *Either/Or* II:202 (II 182), 254 (II 228), 322 (II 289).

[33] Kierkegaard, *Either/Or* II:159 (II 145).

[34] Kierkegaard, *Either/Or* II:42 (II 217).

[35] Kierkegaard, *Either/Or* II:271ff (II 243ff).

[36] Kierkegaard, *Either/Or* II:179-180 (II 162-163).

[37] Kierkegaard, *Either/Or* II:192 (II 173).

[38] Kierkegaard, *Either/Or* II: 208f (II 187f).

[39] Kierkegaard, *Either/Or* II: 163-164 (II 148-149).

[40] MacIntyre, *op. cit.*, p. 54.

[41] MacIntyre is, however, right to emphasize what all too many Kierkegaard scholars, myself included, have failed to stress—namely Kierkegaard's debt to and dialogue with Kant. For an example of a scholar without this blindspot, I refer the reader to Ronald M. Green's *Kierkegaard and Kant: The Hidden Debt* (Albany: SUNY Press, 1992).

[42] For a truly genial page in the hermeneutic of this kind of suspicion consider Kierkegaard's *Sickness Unto Death*, trans. Howard and Edna Hong (Princeton: Princeton University Press, 1980), 48.

[43] See *Søren Kierkegaard's Journals*, trans. and ed. Howard and Edna Hong. assist. by Gregor Malantschuck (Bloomington: Indiana University Press, 1967), 4:509 entries 4895-4896 (X^4 A 350 *n.d.*, 1851, X^4 A 356 *n.d.*, 1851); see also *Journals* 3:407 entry 3091 (X^1 A 680 *n.d.*, 1849); 4:513-514 entry 4900 (X^4 A 569 *n.d.*, 1852).

[44] MacIntyre. *op.cit.*, p. 42.

[45] See, for example, Schopenhauer's *The World as Will and Representation* Vol. I Bk iv, sec. 66, p. 367f in E.J. Payne's translation (New York: Dover, 1969).

[46] Søren Kierkegaard, *Works of Love*, trans. Howard and Edna Hong (Princeton: Princeton University Press, 1995), 151(IX 144).

[47] Kierkegaard, *Journals* 1:398 entry 889 (III A 202 *n.d.*, 1842); see also Kierkegaard's *Either/Or*, II:268-269 (II 241).

[48] Kierkegaard, *Sickness Unto Death* 82 (XI 194).

[49] Matthew 26:11.

[50] Kierkegaard, Works *of Love* 325 (IX 310).

[51] Kierkegaard, *Sickness Unto Death* 82 (XI 194).

CHAPTER 4

DID KIERKEGAARD BELIEVE IN A LIFE AFTER DEATH?

At first glance, this chapter reads as though it were one of many
skirmishes that take place in the battlefield of the journals of
academic philosophy. Nothing, however, could be further from
the truth. Reading Kierkegaard as a proto-Heideggerian, Harrison
Hall claims that for Kierkegaard there was no objective content
to Christianity. More concretely, he argues that the only eternity
that Kierkegaard believed in was on this side of the grave. To put
it in the plainest of terms, Professor Hall finds it impossible to
believe that a figure as brilliant and in some ways as modern as
Kierkegaard could have believed in the Santa Claus like clap-
trap of a hereafter. Professor Hall is not, I think, alone in his
suspicions. Just the opposite, he represents the views of many
students of Kierkegaard and for that matter of people committed to the view that progress and science have, as it were, super-
annuated what used to be regarded as the central tenets of Christianity, say that Jesus was resurrected from the grave and that
Christianly speaking, death is not the end. In that sense, the
following critique of Harrison Hall's important article is addressed
to all those inclined to believe that if Christianity is to survive, it
will only be by virtue of the fact that it has transcended the out-
moded beliefs of the early Christians.

I

Harrison Hall is describing the Kierkegaardian instant as the moment of commitment that makes sense and more of human ex-

istence. The author writes and students of Kierkegaard should not cavil:

> It is from this perspective alone that we can make sense of human existence as temporal rather than simply in time. Instead of a homogeneous series of moments with an arbitrary now-point, we have a sense of the present as decisive and the past and future as significant . . .[1]

In the next paragraph Hall declares that for Kierkegaard, this special conception of the instant is one and the same with the fullness of time 'when the eternal (God) enters time (becomes man) and separates thereby the Old from the New Testament in terms of the possibility of salvation.'[2] Undisturbed, one reads further—'It is the individual's relation to this cultural event that is of real significance.'[3] With an eyebrow now raised, the reader looks for the second clause to explain: 'since salvation is entirely individual and subjective for Kierkegaard.' No one would deny that there is some sense in which salvation must be individual— but entirely subjective? A note after 'Kierkegaard' makes exegetical matters worse: 'for Kierkegaard,' Hall adds, 'there is no objective fact of salvation.'[4]

Now, Kierkegaard and his authors imbue the terms translated 'objective' with more than a half dozen meanings. Given the spatial restrictions endemic to the journal format, one would not expect Mr. Hall to unravel this skein of meanings, and he does not surprise us. Far from it—he proceeds as though 'objective' had a singular and pellucid sense.[5] And what might that be, or more to the polemical point, what does the author mean to write, 'for Kierkegaard there is no objective fact of salvation.' Again, there is no explanation and again no real cause to complain. After all, no scholar should be required to chase after all questions at once; Hall has his own critical agenda and he follows it commendably. By the same token, this reader is within his rights to offer an interpretation of provocative lines left to fare on their own.

The author of 'Love and Death' has said as much, for Kierkegaard there is something that answers to the longing for salvation. There is salvation but no objective fact of it; or again, Christ's word is good—an eternal life awaits us but only, which is not to say 'merely,' in a subjective sense. Agreed, both Climacus and

Kierkegaard emphasize the possibility of an eternal quality of otherwise temporal human life. And apart from this statement of a peculiar fact, salvation in the immanental sense is, as Hall indites, 'subjective'; but the meaningful, workaday life that awaits our commitment is only one aspect of the eternity that Kierkegaard encourages us to long for.

Let us proceed to the issue of contention. Resurrection, a day that is only by analogy a Day of Judgment—these and other promised events are ones that any doubting Thomas or hard-boiled third party can conceive. And if Kierkegaard looked to these events, then there is an objective dimension to his conception of salvation, or in less mincing terms, salvation is not the purely subjective issue that Harrison Hall has him making it out to be. If I have misunderstood then it is a straw man and ultimately myself that I am dragging to court, but where the author foot-notes, 'for Kierkegaard there is no objective fact of salvation,' I read, for Kierkegaard there is no life after death.[6]

Though the textual evidence against his reading is as abundant as it is unequivocal, Harrison Hall is neither the first nor the second commentator to soft-peddle the blind-spot in question. Where otherwise scrupulous scholars turn their heads, missing the gist of meanings otherwise found, one has every reason to wonder, what is the temptation to explain or, where Kierkegaard is presently concerned, what is the offense that will explain the all too egregious error? The very idea of the devil aside, there is no piece of Christian dogma more offensive, i.e., more intellectually repugnant, to modern or, as some would already have it, post-Christian sensibilities than the image cast by creedal terms like these: 'But this I believe, that the resurrection of the dead is at hand, of the just and of ... the unjust.'[7] To be sure, it would be presumptuous of me to suppose that it is because he takes such offense that Hall fails to acknowledge the fairly obvious; and so, the sources of Hall's blind-spot aside, I have heard it remarked[8] that a font of modern wisdom and suspicion such as Søren Kierkegaard could never have rested in the kind of simple-minded hopes expressed in his last graven words:[9]

In yet a little while
I shall have won;
Then the whole fight
Will at once be done.
Then I may rest
In bowers of roses
And perpetually
Speak with my Jesus.

Brorson[10]

And yet, Kierkegaard did rest in just these hopes and in that sense did look forward to a salvation safely labeled, 'objective.'

2

A Kierkegaardian argument can be made to run: where there is commitment there is continuity; and where there is continuity there is something unchanging and where there is something unchanging, there is something outside of time and thus eternal.[11] This, I suppose, is the subjective salvation that Hall leaves Kierkegaard awaiting.

There is direct textual evidence of this realized eschatology. In the *Concluding Unscientific Postscript*, Climacus is busy describing objectivity in terms of the suppression of interest and, alas, as spiritual suicide. In an addendum to the reasoning registered above, we might, for Kierkegaard argue, that where there is no interest, i.e., self-concern, there is no commitment and, again, where there is no commitment, there is no salvation in the immanental sense. N.B., the parenthetical remark:

> The subject's personal, infinite, impassioned interestedness (which is the possibility of faith and then faith, the form of eternal happiness and then eternal happiness)...[12]

The terms of this passage bespeak the fact that, throughout the *Fragments* and *Postscript*, Aristotle is only a whistle away. For everything this side of the Prime Mover, the form of something is its end, actuality, and essence. Accordingly, the interest of the individual is the potential for faith and faith in turn is the form,

and so essence, of eternal happiness. Why then the present com-
plaint?

In the pseudonymous works, and beyond, there is every indi-
cation that faith is its own proof. The true believer who clings to
a certain incertitude with all his heart and mind does not go
without a sign. The definitions are many but under one already
recorded description, faith is an infinite interest in one's existence. This self-concern reaches its natural and true voice in a
self-conscious longing for an eternal happiness.[13] The individual
who turns into this longing assumes a quality of life that some
insist is only born in death. Dying to this world, now and again
taking comfort in the objective thought that, for God, all things
are possible, the subjective thinker finds something of heaven on
earth. This something is the testimony faith receives but does not
demand:

> Consequently, to become subjective should be the highest
> task assigned to every human being, just as the highest reward,
> an eternal happiness, exists only for the subjective person, or
> more correctly, comes into existence for the one who becomes
> subjective.[14]

The thoughts that Kierkegaard dances with are turned this way
and that. The side of the idea he chooses to alight waits upon the
perspective he wishes to convey. Seen from here, faith is decisiveness, from there an expectation, and from another life-view, faith
is trust. It is the same with the nexus of concepts: salvation, eternal
life, immortality. When for one reason and/or another Kierkegaard
wishes to stress the eternal quality of life beyond the grave of the
esthetic, the likes of phrases such as these ring: 'only in the ethical
is there immortality and an eternal life'; 'only in the ethical is your
eternal consciousness'; eternal happiness as the absolute good is
'definable solely in terms of the mode of acquisition'; the eternal
is not something, it is 'higher life' and the germ or first sprout of
this life is ethical consciousness.[15]

Kierkegaard the younger, eternally old man, admonishes—if a
person never learns to sit still, never becomes the immortal
creature that he is, then death will reveal him for the ticket stub
that he was. Barbs like the one quoted below give credence to the
misreading that eternity is, as it were, a state of mind. Climacus

writes that the question of immortality, of everlasting 'continuity'
becomes a jest

> when people who have fantastically dabbled in everything,
> have been everything possible, one day in concern ask the
> pastor whether they will actually remain the same in the
> beyond—after they have not been able in this life to endure
> being the same for a fortnight and therefore have gone through
> all kinds of transmutations. Immortality would admittedly be
> a peculiar metamorphosis if it could trasmute an inhuman
> centipede such as that into the eternal identity with itself,
> which "to be the same" means.[16]

By ignoring parts of the corpus that bear Kierkegaard's own name,
the misguided conclusion is effortlessly reached—eternal life (salvation) is nothing more and, to be sure, nothing less than an
earthly life distinctively qualified. In other, balder terms, there is
no objective fact of salvation - no life after death. Perhaps today,
but most certainly yesterday, this view flies in the face of orthodoxy. Of course, if anyone was able and willing to go against the
theological grain, it was Kierkegaard. But, mind you, it would
have been totally out of character for an author so accustomed to
climbing out on limbs, so concerned with the relationship between his life and words, to have taken this unorthodox stance
in private but not in print. For someone with Kierkegaard's
ego-ideal, reticence on this issue would have been self-understood
as cowardice.

3

I have then assigned myself the rather curious, if not downright
dubious, task of establishing that one long dead once believed in
a life after death. As always, Kierkegaard can be pictured frown-
ing upon his interpreters. If the issue be our own non-being,
then who knows what we are capable of disbelieving, or so
Climacus quips: "For example, what it means to be immortal.
On that topic, I know what people ordinarily know. I know that
some accept immortality, that others say they do not. Whether
they actually accept it, I do not know."[17] But where Kierkegaard
is so personally and profoundly concerned, who is Climacus, the

dialectician in him, to judge? If we take Kierkegaard at his word, the words are there: Kierkegaard believed in a less mundane world, in a more final judgment. Listen to this late journal entry:

> There is something very specific that I have to say, and it weighs so on my conscience that I dare not die without saying it. For the minute I die and leave this world, I will then (as I see it) instantly (so frightfully fast does it happen!) I will then be infinitely far from here, at another place, where even that very second (what frightful speed!) the question will be put to me: Have you carried out your errand, have you very specifically said the specific something you were to say? And if I have not done it what then?[18]

Kierkegaard is religious in his refusal to speculate about the nature of that 'place' and he is quick to chastise those who fail to exercise similar restraint. The proofseeker and day-dreamer are assured immortality is theirs but, note well, continues the theologian with a hammer: 'Immortality is the Judgement. There is not a word more to be said about immortality.'[19] Have no fear, and having no fear live in fear and trembling. These and other assurances form the ground bass of that direct communique, 'The Resurrection of the Just and . . . ': 'Precisely because thou art immortal thou shalt not be able to slip out of God's hand, hide thyself in a grave and pretend that it doesn't matter . . ..'[20]

According to Kierkegaard's counsel, it is a true and good idea to think of this life as a test in the Johannine sense that can be given the term. Lovers of light, lovers of darkness, self-consciously and un-, we will all sit for the exam, we will all reveal ourselves; but fantastic as Kierkegaard admits it seems, that is not the end of it. Unhappy is the man in the valley of his own death, but remember, unhappiest of all is the man who cannot die. In a piece that Hall has searched,[21] Kierkegaard musically repeats, 'for the dead man it is over [*det er forbi*], for the dead man it is over.' No one, save one, can penetrate the silence of the tomb. Ask Lazarus's sister if belief in Christ's afterlife giving powers is incidental to Christian faith.[22] The spiritual watchman urges—if you must know whether or not you are in the fold, ask yourself, do I expect an eternal life?[23] Kierkegaard warns - expect it! The just and, yes, the unjust, will be called from their graves, elsewise, he all but explicitly states, there would be no justice.[24]

Again Kierkegaard believed, which for him is to say "trusted" that Christ had conquered death, spiritual and otherwise. Now, the year is 1854 and Kierkegaard seems acutely aware that his own season is dead winter. He recalls what Bishop Mynster, the family soul-physician once remarked, namely that on Kierkegaard's account the narrow road is closed, we are all doomed—save for Kierkegaard. In a soliloquy meant to be overheard, Kierkegaard exclaims:

> I want some truth here and I want it said honestly, loudly, and clearly. But I do not pretend to be better than the others. Therefore what the old Bishop once said to me is not true - namely, that I spoke as if the others were going to Hell. No, if I can be said to speak at all of going to Hell, then I am going along with them. But I do not believe that; on the contrary, I believe that we will all be saved, I, too and this awakens my deepest wonder.[25]

'We will all be saved,' but from what, a thoroughly esthetic life? Did Kierkegaard really imagine that sooner or later we would all come, or be dragged around and so attain, or by the grace of God be vouchsafed, that subjective sort of salvation he himself otherwise knew as faith? I doubt it, but then again, what is it that we will be saved from? Why, from everlasting death, of course. Even if we did not really have it here, we shall have life in abundance There, or so Kierkegaard felt, with good cause to wonder.

While quote-stringing is a literary activity almost always justifiably deplored, the nature of this exercise demands a bit of it. The scene is once again the *Edifying Discourses*. In a coda to 'The Expectation of Faith,' the magister is expounding upon the words, 'and so let us be saved':

> . . . when like a faithful friend it [the words, 'and so let us be saved'] has accompanied us through all the many relations of life ... has spoken to us warningly and admonishingly, cheerfully and invitingly: that then our soul may be carried away from the world on this last word as it were, to that place where we shall understand its full significance. So we may understand that the same God who by his hand led us through the

world now withdraws it and opens His embrace to receive the
longing soul. Amen.[26]

Literal-minded Kierkegaard was not, but neither is he one to
begin a frothful exegesis the moment all too common, or for
that matter philosophic, sense begins to shudder.[27] For the dogmatic and, I insist, the essential Kierkegaard, both the thought
and event of death are decisive.[28] Once more, after life but not
before, we shall look back upon life and, 'understand its full significance.' Death, or as it seems strange but necessary to say,
'physical death,' is the door to a window on existence that the
living have no ethical business searching for. As early as 1837
Kierkegaard observes, 'when in the final hour it grows dark for a
true Christian, it is because the sunlight of eternal happiness shines
too brightly in his eyes.'[29] Mark you, it is not twilight but dawn,
that is, midnight, or perhaps a minute before; so our much less
than dogmatic keeper of thoughts is scarcely thinking of a forthcoming moment of spiritual bliss; no, the reference is to an eternity in the strictly transcendental sense.[30]

4

Harrison Hall concludes that Heidegger's largely unacknowledged
debt to Kierkegaard is large enough to strain the bounds of what
counts for intellectual debt.[31] While it does not require a sleuth
to detect Kierkegaard's presence in *Sein und Zeit,* it does require
one to track the particular paths of influence down. Masterfully,
Hall has met this requirement and more; but whether the author
aims to or not, his essay insistently invites us to read Kierkegaard
in the reverse, truly backward direction, as though Kierkegaard
were not really a religious author concerned with the problem of
faith for faith's sake, as though Kierkegaard were Heidegger
evangelicized, or an upbuilding author in the Heideggerian mode;
Hall invites:

> There may be some initial resistance to employing the notion
> of love in characterizing Kierkegaard's ideal of authentic
> human existence. Wouldn't Kierkegaard have used the con-
> cept of love rather than faith if that were very close to what he
> meant? I think not. He felt constrained to utilize the

Judeo-Christian conceptual framework. Within that framework, faith was the natural choice for what he had in mind.[32]

That is, are we now to suppose that someone with a healthy
distaste for God can come to Kierkegaard shielded by the dis-
arming thought that where Kierkegaard speaks of faith, it is only
in the service of aiming us toward commitment, authenticity, or
if this be your inoffensive term for the deep, toward, 'ego integ-
rity'?

The terms of Hall's marginalia make it manifest—the assertion
that 'there is no objective fact of salvation' is but an instance of the
broader claim that, for Kierkegaard, 'there is not even any
objective content to Christianity.'[33] In a veritable whisper, Hall
concedes that there is, in fact, an object of appropriation. Again:
'there is not even any objective content to Christianity'; and now
for the whisper - 'none other than the fact that Christ existed.'[34]
Fine, but there is no believing that Christ existed without
believing something about Christ, and what is this something but
a canon of faith or unfaith? The philosopher behind the *Fragments* notwithstanding, there is no bare fact of Christ's existence.
The belief that Christ is or was, is, in the bad sense of the term,
unintelligible without an attending description; and once you
have the description you have the content of Christianity or the
content of its rejection. Why just consider the canonical use that
Anti-Climacus or, for that matter, Kierkegaard makes of the New
Testament. Uncharacteristically, Kierkegaard explains:

> Christianity is to be kept existentially on the move, and
> becoming a Christian is to be made more and more difficult.
> Take a simple example. An officer says to a disorderly mob:
> Move on, please - no explaining. No explaining - why?
> Because he uses authority. Is there, then, nothing objective in
> Christianity or is Christianity not the object of objective
> knowledge? Indeed, why not? The objective is what he is
> saying, he, the authority. But no explaining, least of all the
> kind which, as it were, sneaks behind the back of the authority
> and finally speculates him away too, and turns everything into
> speculation.[35]

In theory, Hall may not disagree, but even where Kierkegaard
once, twice, and thrice underscores the importance of subjectiv-

ity, it is plain that the object of one's belief makes a world of subjective difference. In a famous passage, Kierkegaard loudly hints that it is better to be a true worshipper of false idols than a false worshipper of the true God.[36] But it is understood, there is something infinitely better yet, namely, the true worshipper of the true God. Perhaps a dozen times Johannes defines: *"An objective uncertainty, held fast through appropriation with the most passionate inwardness, is the truth, . . ."*[37] And a few lines later, 'But the above definition of truth is an equivalent expression for faith.' Where there is no objective content there is no uncertainty and so, no faith. In the same tract, faith often appears under the heading 'infinite inwardness.' While he is willing to admit that there is inwardness in madness and paganism alike, even the writer with one toe in the water is clear—there is no infinite inwardness outside the single, unlimiting idea of Christ. More textual arguments can be rolled up to roll the accent on subjectivity back, or at least to its proper Kierkegaardian place. Again, one either trusts in God or his own guiding light, or, as Kierkegaard cautions, faith will have its collision with the understanding. However, push the objective uncertainty too far to the side so that the collision is, who cares how narrowly missed and you volatilize Kierkegaard's conception of faith.

Mind you, and in my best moments mind me, it is not just a question of annulling Kierkegaard's conception of faith. If the New Testament is as offensive as Kierkegaard insists, a monolithic concern with the passional side of faith looms as the next most logical dodge, next after the dodge in the other, objective direction. I am not the one to pontificate—a faith without content is no faith at all, nor is it for me to try and eviscerate Kierkegaard's call to inwardness/subjectivity; there is no quarreling with the advice he has for speculative man: when you think of God, think of sheer subjectivity; or again, when you think of finding faith, concentrate on relating yourself to a Subject, not upon relating a body of propositions to the world, terrestrial or otherwise. But these recommendations are a long way from the pit of a purely subjectivist path.

Yes, Johannes might as well have had it posted—faith does not await salvation, it is salvation. But more frequently than he soothes, Kierkegaard warns, God save the man that God calls. Ask Abraham - faith is murder, i.e., something one might feel inclined to avoid. Yet for all those who work and pray for the strength not to flinch, for all those bent upon living up to the categories wherein one can really speak of 'dangers to the faith,' the belief that what one strives to believe is of no religious moment, poses a danger. The reader is right to remind this author that it is one easy thing to cry, 'here is the mountain,' and quite another to climb, but when embarrassed religiosity ducks in front of all the objective claims it once deemed necessary to stand behind, it runs the risk of becoming abstract, vacuous, and as facile as Kierkegaard assures us the God-relationship is not.

NOTES

[1] Harrison Hall, 'Love and Death: Kierkegaard and Heidegger on Authentic and Inauthentic Human Existence,' *Inquiry* 27 (1984), nos. 2-3, pp. 179-97.

[2] Ibid., p. 185.

[3] Ibid., p. 185.

[4] Ibid., p. 196n.

[5] Ibid., see p. 179.

[6] For a premier example of this waving the question off, see M. Heidegger, *Sein und Zeit* (Tübingen: Max Niemeyer Verlag, 1972), pp. 247-8.

[7] S. Kierkegaard, *Christian Discourses*, trans. Walter Lowrie (Princeton: Princeton University Press, 1971), p. 219.

[8] E.g. Don Cupitt comments, 'The plain man's notion that there is "literally" a life after death... never arises and cannot arise from S.K.'s point of view.' *The Sea of Faith* (London: BBC Publications, 1984), p. 153. Also see, D.A. Phillips, *Death and Immortality* (London: Macmillan Publishing, 1979), pp. 47-49.

[9] As his writings attest, Kierkegaard took his graves and epitaphs very seriously. Indeed, he could, without hyperbole, exclaim:

> There is indeed a shocking eloquence (even though shocking in a different sense than the voice of Abel's blood, which cries out to heaven) when one reads the brief words which a deceased person has had placed over his grave, the last words, his final testament, the last cry, into which he has poured his whole soul. (*Journals and Papers*, trans. and ed. Howard V. and Edna H. Hong [Bloomington: Indiana University Press, 1967], I, p. 334, entry 714.)

[10] See S. *Kierkegaard's Letters and Documents*, trans. Henrik Rosenmeier (Princeton: Princeton University Press, 1978), pp. 26-27. Kierkegaard's last graven words belong to a hymn written by Hans Adolph Brorson (1694-1764). The verse beginning with the words 'Hallelujah! Jeg har min Jesus fundet' was written in 1735 and is number 231 in the Danish Hymnal.

[11] This is the hope-argument written in to the *Concluding Unscientific Postscript* (trans. Howard and Edna Hong (Princeton: Princeton University Press, 1992). Consider, e.g., 306f (VII262f) (Note: following the page reference for any *Postscript* references is the parenthetical reference to the text in the Danish 1st edition).

[12] Kierkegaard, *Concluding Unscientific Postscript* 27 (VII 16).

[13] Kierkegaard, *Concluding Unscientific Postscript* 26 (VII 16), 32 (VII 20) *passim*.

[14] Kierkegaard, *Concluding Unscientific Postscript* 163 (VII 135).

[15] Here and elsewhere I am indebted to Julia Watkin's eye-opening dissertation, *Kierkegaard: Dying and Eternal Life as Paradox* (England: Bristol University, 1979), U.M.I. 83-08721. See esp. pp. 162-97.

[16] Kierkegaard, *Concluding Unscientific Postscript* 146 (VII 146).

[17] Kierkegaard, *Concluding Unscientific Postscript* 171 (VII 141) (emphasis removed).

[18] S. Kierkegaard, *Papers and Journals*, op. cit., VI cit., p. 157.

[19] S. Kierkegaard, *Christian Discourses*, op. cit., p. 213.

[20] Ibid., p. 214.

[21] Namely, 'The Decisiveness of Death,' in *Thoughts on Critical Situations in Human Life* (Minneapolis: Augsburg Publishing, 1941), pp. 75, 115.

[22] Though the reference is to the Resurrection, I am reminded of Wittgenstein's almost confessional note:

> What inclines even me to believe in Christ's Resurrection. ...It is as though I ply with the thought. If he did not rise from the dead, then he decomposed in the grave like any other man. *He is dead and decomposed*. In that case he is a teacher like any other and can no longer *help*; and once more we are orphaned and alone. So we have to content ourselves with wisdom and speculation. We are in a sort of hell where we can do nothing but dream, roofed in, as it were, and cut off from heaven. But if I am to be REALLY saved,—what I need is *certainty*—not wisdom, dreams, or speculation—and this certainty is faith. And faith is faith in what is needed by my *heart*, my *soul*, not my speculative intelligence. For it is my soul with its

passions, as it were with its flesh and blood, that has to be saved, not my abstract mind. (*Culture and Value*, trans. Peter Winch, ed. G.H. Von Wright [Oxford: Basil Blackwell, 1980], p. 33)

[23] S. Kierkegaard, *Edifying Discourses*, trans. David F. and Lillian Marvin Swenson, ed. Paul. L. Holmer (New York: Harper & Row Publishers, 1958), pp. 26 f.

[24] S. Kierkegaard, *Fear and Trembling*, trans. and ed. Howard V. and Edna H. Hong (Princeton: Princeton University Press, 1983), see p. 15; also *The Gospel of Suffering and Lilies of the Field*, trans. David F. and Lillian Marvin Swenson (Minneapolis: Augsburg Publishing, 1948), pp. 19-20.

[25] S. Kierkegaard, *Journals and Papers*, op. cit., I, p. 334, entry 712.

[26] S. Kierkegaard, *Edifying Discourses*, op. cit., p. 28.

[27] For the not so intrepid exegete, Kierkegaard had more than enough harsh words, but look to those in *Fear and Trembling*, op. cit., beginning five lines from the top of p. 72.

[28] Here the decisive turn is ironically tabbed 'a minor event' (*en lille Begivenhed*) but let the reader weigh Anti-Climacus's introductory words: 'Humanly speaking, death is the last of all, and humanly speaking, there is hope only as long as there is life. Christianly understood, however, death is by no means the last of all; in fact, it is only a minor event within that which is all, an eternal life, and, Christianly understood, there is infinitely much more hope in death than there is in life…' (S. Kierkegaard, *The Sickness Unto Death*, trans. and ed. Howard V. and Edna H. Hong [Princeton: Princeton University Press, 1980], pp. 7-80. See also, *Journals and Papers*, op. cit., III, pp. 293-5, entry 2908).

[29] S. Kierkegaard, *Journals and Papers*, op. cit., I, p. 334, entry 712.

[30] Again, my aim has been to establish that Kierkegaard believed in an afterlife. There are philosophical and theological problems (not all of them subtle) with Kierkegaard's concept(s) of salvation that could not be raised, let alone settled, in a reply. But then there is Dr. Watkin's dissertation (see note 12) and Gregor Malantschuk's sovereign analysis in *Kierkegaard's Way to the Truth* (trans. M. Michelsen [Minneapolis: Augsburg Publishing, 1963], ch. V, 'The Problems of the Self and Immortality,' pp. 79-96).

[31] 'Love and Death,' op. cit., p. 196.

[32] Ibid., p. 180.

[33] Ibid., p. 196n.

[34] Ibid., p. 195n.

[35] Kierkegaard, *Journals and Papers*, op. cit., I. p. 75, entry 187.

[36] Kierkegaard, *Concluding Unscientific Postscript* 201 (VII 168).
[37] Kierkegaard, *Concluding Unscientific Postscript* 203 (VII 170).

CHAPTER 5

CAN WE COME TO PSYCHOANALYTIC TERMS WITH DEATH?

Freud's psycho-logic seems to be this: a belief that is without evidence ought to be given up for fantasy, especially if it can be shown to derive from one or another unconscious idea. Too good—and in some perverse cases, too bad to be true, such notions are more likely to mirror a desired reality than reality itself. And so, in *Civilization and its Discontents*[1] an increasingly philosophic Freud exhorts us to stop diverting thought and energy from science by dispensing with devotion to ideas as patently absurd as God and the hereafter.

There are of course philosophical problems more than enough with belief in the afterlife.[2] For example, if there is a personal existence after death it must be a disembodied one, or at least for a time until the end of time when the soul will perhaps be reunited with the body. Many believe that it is plain nonsense to speak about a life that is not the life of some body. Philosophical problems aside, billions have gone into the grave and no one seems to have come out. Freud, is right, objectively speaking we haven't a prayer.

And yet, the true believer who looks forward to an eternal happiness does so only by virtue of his willingness to strain against the understanding. He harbors no illusions about objective thought being on his side. Even more than that, he is likely to concur when a Freud points to a deep and primordial longing as the provenance of his undying trust that death is not the end. Needless to say, the agreement breaks off when the source of the longing itself comes under scrutiny. For unlike a Freud who thinks that the longing is just a childish wish, the one who trusts that death is just the beginning is likely to believe that it was his creator who sowed the seed of this hope. As if we could, Freud's solution is, of course, wherever it is possible to do so without making ourselves psychologically ill, we should renounce our infantile wishes. On that score he had little patience with those perverters of instinct who would die to this world in the hope of finding a place in another.

It does not require an Aristotle to draw out the grim implications of Freud's solution. Surrender the eternal and there immediately looms up the thought that unreasoning hope struggles so valiantly against, namely, death. And as Kierkegaard teaches us, death, or rather our own death is a difficult thought to think.[3] Already I hear some whistler in the dark quip, "Who would want to remain here forever?" But there is no need to answer, for we understand that the sting of death is not that of wanting to remain in this world. And then there is another so thick-skinned as to pretend that death is literally something that we are unable to worry about for where death is we are not. Death is nothing; the imagination must paint something, and so it cannot paint death, which is to pretend that we are kidding ourselves when we think that we are worried about our own demise.[4] If only someone would instruct the imagination that we really cannot imagine death, perhaps, it would give us some rest! But this fantasy is no slave to reason and so we wonder back and forth to the end, each one of us finding something different in the image of ourselves dead. Cut off from the flow, outside history, absolutely and eternally alone—these are some of the shadows that find me stepping across my own grave, and then there is this other.

I am dead awhile or so I imagine. And there in the quiet depths of night my wife sits. Miss me she does, but longing is not the face that looks out from her now. She feels betrayed; much less than the eternal love I vowed, I never think of her any more. "It is worse than that," grief incites. I am not dead in general but dead to her as well. While her pain flames, I remain oblivious. Nothing can spark the thought of her in me. Somehow or other, she takes this insentience for indifference. Doesn't she know that it is absurd to expect concern from a corpse? She does and keens just the same for to her it seems that eternal love has been defeated; that is, revealed to be all-too-temporal. Perish the thought! "No," insists Freud, "perish the hope." But here is the question that is the rub. Can the hope be perished without existing again as hopelessness?

It is one thing to make light of religion's objective claims, having attempted for oneself a solution to the subjective problems that faith is responsive to; and it is another when one has been silenced by those very problems and laughs just the same. There is no doubt that Freud would have us take the half-leap of believing in Death; but to do this correctly, that is, to do it at all, may well require a degree of passion that belongs properly to faith. Once again, death is a difficult thought to think. It becomes especially hard as one becomes what one is and life no longer stretches a boundless sea of possibilities. And when the eleventh hour draws near it becomes harder still.

Now, if Ernest Jones is to be trusted, Freud was more than faithful to the thought of death.[5] Indeed, according to his Boswell, the Master gave too much thought to it. How much is 'too much'? The idea of death crossed Freud's mind at least once a day—and that is too much, or so says the good Doctor Jones. What then were his conclusions? Does Freud offer any advice to make life in this hapless thought more bearable? He does not and yet we would expect Freud, who has otherwise given us what Ricoeur calls "a science of meanings," to have something to say about the meaning of death in life. After all, isn't psychoanalysis unswervingly committed to the project of unearthing the real meaning behind the palimpsestal text of adult mental life? It is almost comic to think of someone offering a catalogue of the kinds of things humans mean and omitting death as though mortal man were not concerned with his mortal lot. No, psychoanalysis must not be allowed to pass, to shrug its shoulders smugly and complain, "What can anyone say about death?"—as if psychoanalysis had never entered the lists of those ready to put false consciousness right. Again, Freud intended to reveal what is really at the back of everyone's mind. Death is there; Erikson agrees:

> [T]he further development of psychoanalysis will have to help us understand and to find fitting terms for the symbolic representation not only of repressed sexuality but also of the ever-present and yet so blatantly denied fact of death in us and around us.[6]

The backward-looking language of psychoanalysis makes the end of life a difficult topic to treat. For Freud the real meaning of our thoughts and expressions comes from within and before—from instinct and personal history. Indeed, if we follow the herd of his followers and ignore Freud's positing of the death instinct,[7] we might conclude that the unconscious, which is arbitrator of our meanings, is itself unconscious of the doom impending upon the less than half-conscious human individual. After all, for the unconscious there is neither time nor extramental reality. Unconsciously speaking, we know nothing of death. The fiction of his death instinct aside, for Freud there is no need for us to take death into account when trying to reveal the self-hidden meanings that write themselves into virtually every form of human communiqué. This, however, is a mistake for it is painfully clear that the idea of death never forgets us.

Psychoanalytic categories make no room for meanings that cannot be recollected and those who live and work in these categories are prone to misunderstand death in their own terms. It is discouraging to learn that even the most exacting efforts to be moral are, at bottom, libidinal. And it is disheartening to hear that a grandiose self-image is the soul of one's striving for perfection. But where death is concerned, it would be reassuring to believe the analyst who explains, "it is not death but something else that troubles you." Whosoever is resolved to work through all unrealistic wishes and so live true to the thought of death must take care to abstain from the succor of such explanations for these explanations must be reckoned as vehicles for the repression of the very idea that we intended to face. If our belief in the afterlife is simply an expression of our fear of death then there can be no denying the belief without coming to terms with the forces that gave rise to it. Whereas, Kierkegaard, the depth psychologist with different categories up his sleeve, gave us notes on the lessons that death could teach us, Freud and his followers are strangely reticent about the significance of the idea that they would have us accept.

NOTES

[1] Sigmund Freud, *Civilization and its Discontents* (1930), standard Ed., Vol. XXI (London: Hogarth Press, 1957), 84-85 and *passim*. See also Freud's *Future of an Illusion* (1927), standard Ed., Vol. XXI, pp. 46-50.

[2] St. Paul himself raises some of these philosophical questions. See I Corinthians, chapter 15.

[3] For a wonderful passage on this difficulty, see Climacus's answer to the question, What does it mean to die? *Concluding Unscientific Postscript,* pp. 165-171

[4] Thomas Nagel provides a lucid and informative response to the question, Should we worry about our own death? See his *Mortal Questions,* Cambridge Univ. Press, 1979 pp. 1-10.

[5] Jones, E *The Life and Work of Sigmund Freud*, Vol. III (New York: Basic Books, 1957), 279.

[6] E. H. Erikson, *Life History and the Historical Moment* (New York: Norton, 1975) 159.

[7] This is not to say that going beyond the pleasure principle is any solution to the problem—how am I to live with my own inexorable death? Quite the contrary, I follow Ernest Becker who interprets this theoretical gambit as yet another symptomatic expression of the denial of death: "The fiction of death as an 'instinct' allowed Freud to keep the terror of death outside his formulations as a primary human problem of ego mastery... In this formulation, it is not a general human problem, much less the primary human problem, but it is magically transformed, as Rank so succinctly put it, 'from an unwished-for necessity to a desired instinctual goal'" (*The Denial of Death* [New York: Free Press], 99).

CHAPTER 6

KIERKEGAARD CONTRA FREUD: ON THE PROPER SCOPE OF OUR MORAL ASPIRATIONS

I. A CAVEAT TO THE AUTHOR

In the chapter to follow I shall have Kierkegaard defending what could justly be termed a "rigorist" ethical position. Naturally, this will involve a defense of Kierkegaard. But anyone who knows Kierkegaard's articles in the "Fædreland" knows that he was harsher with his would-be protectors than he was with his critics. As though every apologist were *de facto* a Judas![1] Since Kierkegaard is not here to defend himself against the likes of this Kierkegaard apologist, let me direct a few admonitory words to myself.

There is, I have come to judge, a type of person whose first and second impulses are to applaud, recommend, and write apologies for almost any rigorist position. Now, anyone who has an eye for children will soon observe that there are some thoughts that a child quite simply and immediately enjoys. And if, in the course of conversing with a child you chance upon one of these amusement parks, the child's eyes will alight, and he will beseech you to "say that again." As Freud taught, it is not much different with adults. For reasons that go beyond our justifications, each of us has an almost natural fondness for certain kinds of ideas. Rigorist ideas seem to be one of mine; which is not to commit the genetic fallacy of concluding that therefore all my demanding thoughts are false, but it is, I think, to warn something.

Kierkegaard insisted that a person's life ought to be understood as saying something about his words. More specifically, he often suggests that a person who does not live up to his ideals does not really understand them. And when Kierkegaard judged that his own ideas were not expressed in the medium of his actions he signed his written expressions with a pseudonym. But if Kierkegaard needed a pseudonym to make the Abrahamic pronouncements that he did, I could use a pseudonym to interpret Kierkegaard.

Against those who would level moral ideals to psychological capacities, my Kierkegaard argues that where the ethical is concerned we are never justified in excusing ourselves as unable: unwilling, and so guilty, yes, but never unable. But this unconditionalism amounts to announcing that where ethics is concerned, conditions and consequences are of no consequence, or at least not for the individual individually holding court with his conscience. And yet as often as such Kantian ideas are bandied about, who really is Ahab enough to abide by the view that even if it means your own death, or the death of your loved ones, you have to do what you have to do, and that is it? Not long ago, I attended a talk by a prominent scholar who offered an impassioned defense of the idea that it is always wrong to lie, no matter what. The audience was visibly moved. Then one fellow stood up and pressed, "Do you mean to say that that Swedish fellow who by deception saved the lives of perhaps 100,000 Jews only to lose his own life, did something wrong." Seemingly delighted, the moral rigorist answered, "Yes, he was wrong." The cross-examiner waved his hand, quipped, "That's madness" and sat down. Our scholar went on to try and explain but he had lost his listeners.

Apropos of moral rigorism, Kierkegaard judged Kant to be wrong; reason alone cannot keep us from cutting and running before the kinds of self-sacrifices that moral reason should daily put before us. We could never be strict enough with ourselves to bind ourselves to the law we supposedly give ourselves. Kierkegaard states:

> There must be some compulsion, if it is to be a serious matter. If I am not bound by anything higher than myself, and I am to bind myself, where would I acquire the rigorousness as A by which, as B, I am to be bound, so long as A and B are the same.[2]

In other words, rigorism is only possible with the help that is the fear of God.

The person who insists upon keeping moral perfection as the moral norm has to keep a third eye on himself, to make certain that he really believes what he pretends to believe, to make certain that he really is always striving to measure up to the standard he rather strangely insists upon torturing himself with. Far more often than not the tendency is to try to have it both ways, rigorism in posture and meliorism in practice. In fact, it was just this kind of hypocrisy, this preaching of Christian ideals and shoving Jews into the streets, that made Freud more than a little suspicious of high-mindedness. But the trick of keeping your absolutes and conditions at the same time is, I think, most routinely accomplished by cloaking oneself in a chronic, but largely nominal, that is, largely toothless, sense of guilt. The other side of this cloak is admiration, concerning which Kierkegaard reminds all ethical enthusiasts that "Ethically understood, there is nothing on which one sleeps so soundly as on admiration over an actuality."[3] Standing at attention before such and such a thought, and in admiration before the Bonhoeffer who embodies that thought, one imagines that he has embraced the ideal which, in the stillness of his admiration, he is actually departing from every step as quickly as the meliorist he frowns upon. But the telling difference is that this nominal guilt and admiration enable the nominal rigorist to retain a nostalgic relationship to certain ordering ideals, a relationship which more self-consciously pragmatic folk may or may not have painfully broken off.

2. On the question of moral capacities

Freud, the moralist, was not one for providing much in the way of explicit moral advice. He was, after all, much less than sanguine about the prospects for directly influencing life from the top down. It is, Freud believed, only an elite few who can make their instincts listen to reason. More to the point, it is not the ego, not I, who decides how I am going to read the law within me, so pure arguments about that law are not likely to change it one way or the other. Conscience is the billboard for deeply un-conscious processes, and there is no simple deciding to change the message on the billboard.

Nevertheless, truly reluctant as he seems to have been, Freud did eventually become a philosopher, and a moral one at that. Following his beloved Schopenhauer, Freud urged us to adopt more realistic ideals. In *Civilization and its Discontents*, everyone with enough ego autonomy to listen is explicitly urged to lower his or her moral ideals to psychological realities:

> [W]e are very often obliged, for therapeutic purposes, to oppose the super-ego, and we endeavour to lower its demands. Exactly the same objections can be made against the ethical demands of the cultural super-ego. It, too, does not trouble itself enough about the facts of the mental constitution of human beings. It issues a command and does not ask whether it is possible for people to obey it. On the contrary, it assumes that a man's ego is psychologically capable of anything that is required of it, that his ego has unlimited mastery over his id. This is a mistake; and even in what are known as normal people the id cannot be controlled beyond certain limits. If more is demanded of a man, a revolt will be produced in him or a neurosis, or he will be made unhappy.[4]

Setting to the work of opposing the super-ego, Freud argued that Christ may as well have commanded us to fly as to command universal love. Despite what Jesus may have thought, there is simply not enough libido to go around, and so you cannot (and ought not) try to love others as you love yourself.[5] The old pleas of "impossible" have of course been ringing for centuries, but with Freud we are invited to think that there is scientific evidence that conscience does not necessarily know what it is talking about. But beyond physical impossibility, there is another suggested sense in which the Good could be written off for not taking the facts about our mental constitution into account—and that sense is written into the last line of the text cited above. An ideal is too ideal if living within it produces either illness or unhappiness.

Freud' s prescription is plain, the modern individual ought to bring his moral vision down a few pegs. As for which pegs, Freud was quite specific—certain Christian ideals ought to be sacked, e.g., love thy neighbor as thyself, or, more fantastic and destructive yet, love thy enemy as thyself. But that is not all, given the inevitability of the itch we are all born into, and the energy it requires to keep from scratching we ought, hinted Freud, to modify the hyperbolic demands of monogamy. Freud's formula is clearly, adjust your oughts to your cans.

Like Hume on religious conviction, Freud philosophized that where there is no scientific question of truth, we ought to allow the effects to decide. If, for example, belief in Christian ethics produces morally uplifting effects, then let the illusion it is grounded upon be. Freud preached, "The most important thing is to endure."[6] If the task be to make yourself a less edgy citizen, and an image of a suffering servant will help you to control your aggressions then, by all means, keep your images. However, the trouble as Freud perceived it was that reaction formations make for very poor shepherds. The Jansenists of the world will make us more, not less nervous and the more nervous we are, the more and worse the moral transgressions.

While every child of the therapeutic accepts the conclusion, no intellectual grandchild of Freud would today even think of putting the leveling argument in these old orthodox Freudian terms. Still, the argument for moral/psychological realism is as follows: the process of repression rests upon a transfer of destructive instincts to the super-ego, the higher the cultural ideal, the greater the repression; the greater the repression the greater the destructive force appropriated to the super-ego and the greater the destructive force of the super-ego, the nastier the super-ego; and the nastier the super-ego, the nastier the citizen feels and acts.[7] If you are suspicious of all this, just look in the mirror, or the clinic, or as Freud did when he made this observation: consider humanity at war. "We are living beyond our psychological means,"[8] tallies the treasurer of moral means, and the result is not only the implosion of bad conscience but an explosive capacity for instant inhumanity.

For Freud, morality equals law, that is, if moral theorists are rightfully concerned with anything, it is with articulating the rules which will enable people to get along as painlessly as possible. And given those guiding prejudices, it is no wonder that Freud chuckled over ethical theorists and other flagellants who squint over their intentions.

> The impulses of another person are naturally hidden from our observation. We deduce them from his actions and behavior, which we trace to motives born of his instinctual life. Such a conclusion is bound to be, in many cases, erroneous. This or that action which is 'good' from the civilized point of view may in one instance be born of a 'noble' motive, in another not so. Ethical theorists class as 'good' actions only those which are the outcome of good impulses; to the others they refuse their recognition. But society, which is practical in its aims, is little troubled on the whole by this distinction; it is content if a man regulates his behavior and actions by the precepts of civilization, and is little concerned with his motives.[9]

Who knows, and who cares what your intentions are, so long as you pay your taxes and do not lie, cheat, or steal too often? However, beyond obedience to the laws, and that which is required of me to keep up my chosen contracts of love, nothing can reasonably be demanded. Not surprisingly Freud thought St. Francis unreliable[10] and, if you press them, the clients of Freud's disciples' students will tell you something similar about Mother Theresa. After all, how are they to make sense of the injunction, or worse yet of people who obey the injunction, to give everything to the poor? If Schweitzer is a saint, what does that make me, and so on and so forth rumbles the moral preconscious. Like Aristotle, Freud did not even bother to argue that there can be no real question of being obliged to sacrifice, or for that matter of being obliged to be willing to sacrifice, one's prospects for happiness. Ethics (read: "law/society") may rightfully demand an individual's life, but when duty demands giving up happiness it shows that duty has gone mad. I suppose the demand to set one's life aside, to take care of one's parents, could be made the subject of a cruelty plea not unlike the one which Freud tenders concerning sexual mores, but this is not the place to try and drag a moral creed out of Freud's heirs. It is, however, the page to consider a fundamental turn in his moral reasoning, and that turn is Freud's to repeat. Ethics makes drafts upon our psychological means and, as such, it had better be realistic, it had better keep abreast of its accounts, for those accounts are limited.

On any given matter, the call to psychological realism, is an excellent method for eliciting a melange of opinions. For instance, Kierkegaard would be the first to concede that where morals are concerned psychological realism is just what we need.11 Indeed, from one end of the corpus to the other, Kierkegaard can be caught smiling at earlier ethicists,[12] and in particular at the Greeks, for showing so little awareness of what each of us is up against in ourselves. Clearly, anyone interested in fighting the good fight must know who he is grappling with. And how might I come to that self-knowledge? Resistant to the thought as he claimed everyone was bound to be, one psychologist seldom accused of being naive has it that it is only by a revelation from God that I can come to understand what a failed understanding might call the irrational in me.[13] This same psychologist has a premonitory word for those of us who, armed with idea that we ought not demand the impossible of ourselves, feel tempted to shave our moral standards down to size. The author of *The Concept of Anxiety* warns:

> The more ideal ethics is, the better. It must not permit itself to be distracted by the babble that it is useless to require the impossible for even to listen to such talk is unethical, and something for which ethics has neither time nor opportunity. Ethics will have nothing to do with bargaining....[14]

And if it be unethical to listen to such talk from someone else, it must be unethical to listen to oneself mulling over the leveling idea. But what a heretical thought in postmodernity, namely, that it is a transgression just to encourage oneself to think along certain lines!

For Kierkegaard, the transgressions which the sin-blinkered mind takes alone to be sins are very often acts that follow, though not exactly of necessity, from states which we preconsciously work ourselves up or down into. This is the lost wisdom of suppression, and as such it must ring as an anathema to all true, though perhaps much more than yesterday, discreet believers in the ethos of abreaction, an ethos which all too glibly assures that while you may be responsible for your deeds, you cannot be tried for what you think and feel.

But again are some ideals too ideal? As Kierkegaard writes it, it is not only unethical but unreasonable (babble) to think that since it is impossible to be perfectly faithful to one's spouse, it is permissible to philander once every ten years.

Kant held half of Kierkegaard's reasons for maintaining that the ideality of ethics be maintained against all cries to the effect that the standard is too high. As I understand some of those pangs of ethical theory, Kant believed that once we begin judging our moral laws in terms of our capacities, performing one's duty will become a talent for the lack of which one simply cannot be blamed. Well steeped in his Kant, Kierkegaard comments:

> In the realm of genius, the realm of natural qualifications, the realm of the aesthetic, what counts is: to be able. In the realm of the ethical: to be obliged. Therefore the ethical is related to the universally human; whereas the aesthetic is related to the difference between man and man. It would be a contradiction of the ethical to speak of *being obliged* if every human being did not have the conditions for being able if he himself only wills.[15]

When a Freud becomes a Solon, there won't be any psychological need to run the uncomfortably good Samaritan through a battery of psychological tests and explanations. No, let us appoint the Good Joe who devotes his life to the poor an ethical genius, and consider ethically gifted anyone who does eight hours plus of volunteer work each week. There is, however, more than one problem with this curved grading system. If the moral law only applies to people with certain talents, then it is not universalizable. And so, for the narcissist who really cannot help but relate to others as objects there will be blanket excuses. But that is less than half of it: contrary to Kant's designs, a conditional law does not hold at every moment; therefore, if Freud's psychological realism triumphs we can look forward to many a moral holiday a la: I cannot really blame myself for verbally abusing my wife for I was under terrible stress, and besides, some of her remarks activated very unnerving, archaic feelings. Once again, Kant maintained that morality requires the adoption of some principle of choice, namely, a maxim which will prohibit endless fluctuations in the direction of the will. However, once conscience has its conditions, something other than the moral law becomes arbiter of choice, and so the mincing will once again begin to flap in the wind.[16]

Kant in *Religion within the Limits of Reason*,[17] and Kierkegaard from first to last, meant to make it plain that there is no moral middle way. The claim that the standards we pretend to try and live by are too high and so nothing but fuel for a morally unproductive sense of guilt is an attempt to plow the narrow path into a broad and middle one. Kierkegaard held that there is nothing between either and or. The individual who takes the Good to be being good on balance has a paltry conception of the Good and correspondingly a paltry will—which is for Kierkegaard to say, a paltry self. According to Kierkegaard's map, the position between duty and self-love, which Freud's would have us searching out, stands right on the spot called "double-mindness":

> The double-minded person stands at the crossroads.... [H]e believes that he has discovered that there is a third road—and it is along this road he is walking.
>
> This third road has no name since it does not exist at all, and thus it is unexplainable that he, especially if he is to be honest, cannot say which road he is taking....
>
> And how, then, does he proceed along this third road, which is narrower than an acrobat's tightrope, since it does not exist at all? Does he go along smoothly and steadily like someone who has a definite goal before his eyes...? No, he walks that way only on the road of the good—with only the good before his eyes. Or does he walk along like someone who pursues every pleasure on the broad highway of desire? No, he is not walking that way either....
>
> He walks very slowly.... He feels his way with his foot, and when he finally puts his foot down and takes a step, he promptly looks at the clouds to see from which direction the wind is coming and whether the smoke is rising straight up from the chimney.[18]

The image here is the image Philip Rieff casts of the Therapeutic, an image of a prudent and stoically calculating, if not self-manipulating individual. Prudence was not exactly Kierkegaard's portrait of good willing, "but that," some will say, "is Magister Kierkegaard's problem." And in truth, more than Prudence insists: let Kierkegaard show us what is wrong with prudence, or, more specifically, what is wrong with living up to our ego ideals by moving them down a bit.

To begin with, Kierkegaard does not think the leveling will end after the first sale. If Kierkegaard is any prophet, once the downscaling begins it will go from stealing is not so bad to stealing is a virtue. In a journal entry pointing to the democratization of Denmark and the revolution in France, Kierkegaard warns:

> Through incessant voting ethical concepts will ultimately vanish from the race. The power of ethical concepts is the context of conscience; but voting externalizes everything. Many people still live in the comfortable idea that the world will never get so bad that stealing, for example, becomes a virtue. Who knows that? Look at France![19]

A peek at Kierkegaard's journals will immediately reveal that by 1850 he was more than a little piqued about political events in quietly revolutionary Denmark, and in particular about the ascension to the throne of the great steamrolling abstraction he called, "The Public" (Publikum). But the complex issue of his political views aside,[20] Kierkegaard insists that once Freud's assumptions become accepted, once ethics and public law become the indistinguishable province of policemen, conscience (inwardness) will vanish, and then who knows—perhaps the Crown's former subjects will "hang the king with the intestines of the last priest."

Though he himself was a great believer in the not so primal horde's trampling capacity, there is, thought Freud, little danger that the authority, hopefully within us, will be voted into extinction. But again, the thrust of Freud's challenge to so-called rigorist ethics is that by common standards moral rigorism produces more moral transgressions than less harsh super-egos. Kierkegaard never placed much moral weight on what may end up looking something like crime statistics. Not much weight is, for Kierkegaard, too much: "Just as metaphysics has supplanted theology, it will end with physics supplanting ethics. The whole modern statistical approach to morality contributes to this."[21] But Kierkegaard's apocalypses ignored, the overall behavior of a society is the acknowledged proof or disproof of Freud's pudding.

As I have already suggested, at this level the choice between exalted and not so exalted ideals pretends to be an empirical question. Which is the better means to the end of a more civilized society? If, for realistic instance, there is one society with neither much spirit nor much crime but a fair share of smiles, then are the dictates of that society's conscience better or worse than another in which many are driven to both neurosis and acting out (transgression), but a few are chosen to become individuals in the Kierkegaardian sense? My query is, of course, ridiculous, but this line of quasi-moral reasoning is, I think, the only one which a Freud would feel compelled to consider.

3. On the question of guilt

Kierkegaard's square one is plain pathology for Freud, and for Kierkegaard the realization of psychoanalytic concepts of health is almost a sure sign that the sickness unto death has taken a turn for the worse. So entirely different are their guiding premises that, even where they speak to the same point it is difficult to make them speak to one another. Freud's written words can be interpreted as saying, Why not bring our criterion for being a person down to earth? To which an eviscerated Kierkegaard could, I suppose, be made to reply that while the old standards make us feel low they provide a sense of meaning. But from his letter to Princess Bonaparte, we know what Freud thought of the thirst for meaning:

> The moment one inquires about the sense or value of life, one is sick since objectively neither of them has any existence.[22]

Unlike his Judge Wilhelm, Kierkegaard was no believer in Pascal's Wager Argument. He would have been the last one to advocate commitment to high ideals as a form of therapy, and so we stumble upon the dividing line again—what has Kierkegaard to say to the moralist in Freud? On the decisive issue of the morally debilitating effects of guilt, Kierkegaard would say that Freud was partially right. There is indeed a form of guilt that issues in objective grounds for guilt. Not that I think Freud wrote to abolish guilt, just to demythologize it. As Kierkegaard's foremost Christian psychologist Anti-Climacus observes,[23] guilt over sin produces sin, and sin guilt and guilt sin, and so on and so forth. However, for Kierkegaard it is not the standard itself that goads us into whipping ourselves with the standard. It is not the Good's fault when as the mantra goes, "we feel badly about ourselves." The individual who strains so hard at trying to become a saint that he explodes (Freud's example) has himself, and probably his pride to blame. Spiritually speaking, the kind of guilt, the kind of self-torment and rebellion that Freud seems to equate with all guilt is a sinful sinking of oneself in the feeling of guilt.[24]

Kierkegaard takes us to be both much less than passive and much less than guiltless in this truly destructive suffering from guilt. Psychologically speaking, Kierkegaard takes another step in what may well be the direction of the perverse. The further step: those of us who make others suffer becaue of our own self-hatred ought to repent, as opposed to hating ourselves for hating ourselves.[25] It is as though there are right ways and sinful ways of feeling guilt; or it is as though there were a real and false consciousness of being a sinner, where the former does not lead to the self torment that so torments the children of Freud, but to the repentant resolve to sin no more. But the mirror that measures everyone by the standard he chooses, is a mirror that threatens to cheat us out of repentance, by binding us in a spiritually deadly, false self-knowledge. So what does Kierkegaard have to say to the conscious and unconscious followers of Freud? That for the sake of a true sin-consciousness, for the sake of being open to grace, we ought to keep our super-egos right where Christ commanded them to be—breathing demands for the impossible down our necks? If only for the sake of the communicator, such things need to be said: even if it be to stones, or as orthodoxy talking to itself. But no true believer is likely to be threatened by Freud's insinuations that the Good Shepherd did not know his sheep. Conversely, the atheist is not going to agree to demand Christ of himself for the sake of repentance. What, after all, would Kierkegaard have to say to the individual who announces that he knows himself well enough to know that he is unable instead of guilty?

Or more gravely yet, how would he respond to the person who may do what he thinks he can, but otherwise has seen enough of himself to seal the whole question of his moral aspirations, though he can almost imagine someone else, someone younger, earnestly addressing the question.

4. AN ETHICAL EVASION

In response to a sense of moral crisis, there is today, a great deal of clamor for more ethics education. I do not think that Kierkegaard would have been sympathetic to calls for more ethics instruction. He did not think that our moral problems were the result of a lack of knowledge or acumen in analyzing ethical issues. On Kierkegaard's reckoning, we know what is up, and the task is to hold on to that knowledge, to resist talking ourselves out of what we know. At the end of what amounts to Kierkegaard's response to the problem of *akraisa*, he has his favorite alter-ego, Anti-Climacus, explain:

> . . . this is how perhaps the great majority of men live: they work gradually at eclipsing their ethical religious comprehension, which would lead them out into decisions and conclusions that their lower nature does not much care for...[26]

Sin is ignorance, but an ignorance that we are responsible for producing. But what is the motive? What is so unthinkable about the Good? What are the decisions and conclusions that our lower natures do not much care for?

Both Freud and Kant agree that the moral life is essentially internal combat. Kierkegaard concurs that the ethical, the universally human, that which separates us from the beast in us, is the willingness to let go of ourselves; in other words, self-denial in the non-prudential or non-aesthetic application of that term. But more than knowing or having once known what we ought to do, Kierkegaard implies that we have some discomforting sense of what this knowledge requires—hence the disturbing conclusions we do not much care for. Cleave to the mast of any principle and you will soon enough be out over the deep. Take something as trivial as resolving to refrain from all gossip and within a few days if not hours you will be likely to offend someone with your sanctimonious airs. Take almost any principle and hold to it firmly, and in no time the dialogue between knowing and willing will begin. In no time you will be trying to convince yourself that your principled stance, say, never to lie, is really psychological rigidity and that you ought to loosen up, scale down, and what's the difference if every now and then you call in sick when you are well. Probably none at all, and that is why Kierkegaard somewhat queerly emphasizes that the ethical requires imagination, the imagination to disturb your life over matters about which the world is not going to disturb you.

On the grand scale, it may be that Kierkegaard measures out as a relatively minor philosopher, but he was non pareil as a moral phenomenologist. And according to the moral phenomenologist, we have a clear enough idea of where our ideals will take us and do not much want to go there. This being the case, psychological realism would suggest that there might be something akin to defenses against the Good, or, as Kierkegaard terms them, "ethical evasions." Not sometimes but often times, it is comforting to imagine discovering that our higher motives are our false ones, and it can be a balm to think that we haven't the capacity to do what we have no inclination to do. As Kierkegaard tells it, the wishfulfilling scenario is to imagine good willing to be a talent, and then to judge yourself highly unable. Kierkegaard notes, "Just as one wants to be praised for his humility when he is not a genius and does not aspire to be one, so we want to be praised also for humility because we are humble enough to be satisfied with ethical shabbiness."[27] Squeezed between guilt and self-sacrifice, we have every strong motive for turning to psychology as a vehicle of repression. For, as Kierkegaard exposes us:

> There is nothing of which every man is so afraid as getting to know how enormously much he is capable of—do you want to know? You are capable of living in poverty; you are capable of enduring almost all possible mistreatment, etc. But you do not wish to get to know this; no, you would become enraged at the person who would tell you this, and you regard as a friend only the one who will help you to confirm yourself in the idea, I am not capable of enduring, it is beyond my power.[28]

Or as Freud says, it is "beyond my psychological means."[29]

NOTES

[1] See Søren Kierkegaard, *Sickness Unto Death*, trans. and ed. Howard and Edna Hong (Princeton: Princeton University Press, 1980), 87 (XI 198). (Note: following every Hong edition page reference is the page reference of the quote or section from the Danish 1st edition or the Papirer.)

[2] See *Søren Kierkegaard's Journals and Papers*, trans. and ed. Howard and Edna Hong, assist. by Gregor Malantschuck (Bloomington: Indiana University Press, 1967), I:76 entry 188 (X²A 396 n.d., 1850). This is an amended version of the Hong translation. See also Louis Mackey's commentary on this passage in his *Points of View: Readings of Kierkegaard* (Tallahassee: Florida State University Press, 1986), 31-32.

[3] Søren Kierkegaard, *Concluding Unscientific Postscript*, trans. and ed. Howard and Edna Hong (Princeton: Princeton University Press, 1992), 360 (VII 312).

[4] Sigmund Freud, *Civilization and its Discontents*, (1930), standard edition (London: Hogarth Press, 1957), 21:74. See also 138-42.

[5] Freud, *Civilization and its Discontents* 56f. Also, for an analysis of Freud's theory of love that conflicts at points with my own, see E. Wallwork's superb "Thou Shalt Love thy Neighbor As Thyself: The Freudian Critique," *Journal of Religious Ethics* 10: 269.

[6] Sigmund Freud, "Thoughts for Times on War and Death (1915)," in *Collected Papers,* ed. E. Jones, trans. J. Riviere (New York: Basic Books, 1959), 4:317.

[7] Sigmund Freud, "The Economic Problem in Masochism," in *Collected Papers* 2: 266-67. See also, idem. *The Ego and the Id* (1930), trans. J. Riviere, ed. J. Strachey (New York: Norton & Co., 1960), 39-41.

[8] Freud, "Economic Problem of Masochism" 267.

[9] Freud, "Thoughts on War and Death" 298.

[10] Freud, *Civilization and its Discontents* 49.

[11] In the *Papirer* Kierkegaard notes, "Psychology is what we need, and above all, expert knowledge of human life and sympathy with its interests" (5:B53:119).

[12] Søren Kierkegaard, *Concept of Anxiety*, trans. Reidar Thomte (Princeton: Princeton University Press, 1980), 16-17 (IV 288-289); idem. *Sickness Unto Death* 90 (XI 201).

[13] Kierkegaard, *Sickness Unto Death* 96 (XI 207), *passim.*

[14] Kierkegaard, *Concept of Anxiety* 17 (IV 289).

[15] Kierkegaard, *Journals and Papers* 1:426 entry 975 (X^1 A 430 n.d., 1850).

[16] I am much indebted to Ronald M. Green for his insights concerning Kant's influence on Kierkegaard. For an excellent discussion of the relationship between these two thinkers see R.M. Green's *Kierkegaard and Kant: The Hidden Debt* (Albany: SUNY Press, 1992).

[17] Immanuel Kant, *Religion within the Limits of Reason*, trans. T.M. Green and H.H. Hudson (New York: Harper and Row, 1960). Cited on page 155 of R.M. Green's *The Hidden Debt*.

[18] Søren Kierkegaard, *Purity of Heart Is to Will One Thing* in *Upbuilding Discourses in Various Spirits*, trans. and ed. Howard and Edna Hong (Princeton: Princeton University Press, 1993), 41-42 (VII 148-149).

[19] Kierkegaard, *Journals and Papers* 1:430 entry 986 (X^2 A 419 n.d., 1850).

[20] For a superb treatment of this topic see Bruce Kirmmse's *Kierkegaard in Golden Age Denmark* (Bloomington: Indiana University Press, 1990).

[21] Kierkegaard, *Journals and Papers* 1:408 entry 927 (VII^1 A 15 n.d.,1846).

[22] Sigmund Freud, *Complete Psychological Works*, trans. and ed. J. Stachey (London: Hogarth Press, 1953) 24 Vols., 18:252.

[23] Kierkegaard, *Sickness Unto Death* 105f (XI 215f).

[24] Kierkegaard, *Sickness Unto Death* 110f (XI 220f).

[25] For a splendid treatment of this subject see Ronald F. Marshall's "News from the Graveyard: Kierkegaard's Analysis of Christian Self-Hatred" in *Pro Ecclesia*, Vol. ix, No. 1, pp. 19-41.

[26] Kierkegaard, *Sickness Unto Death* 110f (XI 220f).

[27] Kierkegaard, *Journals and Papers* 2:293 entry 1802 (XI^1 A 130 n.d., 1854).

[28] Kierkegaard, *Journals and Papers* 1:440 entry 1007 (XI^2 A 381 n.d., 1854-55).

[29] An early version of this paper was presented at a faculty seminar at the Chicago Institute for Psychoanalysis, February 24, 1988.

CHAPTER 7

MAKING THE DARKNESS VISIBLE: ON THE DISTINCTION BETWEEN DESPAIR AND DEPRESSION IN KIERKEGAARD'S *Journals*

Kierkegaard used to complain that "the age of making distinctions is passed."[1] The age of making the distinction between despair and depression is certainly passed. Indeed, were someone today to say that he was in despair, we would almost surely think that what he really meant to say was that he was depressed. No doubt the demise of despair has something to do with the collapse of sacred order.[2] It used to be that despair was considered one of the seven deadly sins, inasmuch as the despairing individual was considered to be giving up on God. Today, despair is understood to be hopelessness, hopelessness to be depression, and depression to be something that you treat as Kierkegaard puts it, *mit Pulver und mit Pillen,*[3] that is, by throwing pills at it. Still, I have at times sensed some dissatisfaction with the present tendency to read every pang of the psyche as a symptom of an illness most frequently understood as a "chemical imbalance." Kierkegaard gave much thought to the meaning of mental anguish and his meditations on this subject should speak to an age in which most people will, at some point in their lives, seek out professional help for psychological problems, most commonly for depression.

In this chapter I will examine Kierkegaard's thoughts on the relation between depression and despair. Kierkegaard's published writings on depression are, for the most part, written into his pseudonymous texts, *Stages on Life's Way, Repetition*, and *Either/ Or*. There have been a number of commentaries[4] on the proto-theories contained in these works, but scant attention has been paid to Kierkegaard's own self-observations regarding what he termed his "thorn in the flesh"[5] or depression.[6] I will focus on the introspective soundings that Kierkegaard takes in his journals, for it is, I believe, in these pages that Kierkegaard offers the most light on the difference between the night of the psyche and the night of the spirit.

From the first to the last page of his life, Kierkegaard dragged the ball and chain of his melancholy around. Like Pascal, Montaigne and other keepers of the invisible darkness, Kierkegaard watched his depression with the eye of a naturalist, and like more modern psychological men and women, he kept copious notes on his sorrow. Through hundreds of entries there are a number of recurrent themes. For one, that he was in unspeakable and chronic mental anguish. By his own account, Kierkegaard's depression was severe enough to bring him to the razor's edge. In 1836 he made the following journal entry:

> I have just returned from a party of which I was the life and soul; witticisms poured from my lips, everybody laughed and admired me—but I left, yes, the dash should be as long as the radii of the earth's orbit————————————————
>
> ———————————————————————————
>
> and wanted to shoot myself.[7]

This self-revelation hints at the theme of hiddenness, which is explicit in other journal entries. One of the fixed points in Kierkegaard's authorship is his claim that the inner and outer are incommensurable.[8] For Kierkegaard, you cannot read the liniments of a person's spiritual life off from his actions. There are hints of this anti-Hegelian precept in Kierkegaard's notes on his melancholy. Over the years, he alternately gloats and moans about his ability to conceal both the fact and content of his psychological suffering:

> People have continually done me indescribable wrong by continually regarding as pride that which was intended only to keep the secret of my melancholy. Obviously, I have achieved what I wanted to achieve, for hardly anyone has ever felt any sympathy for me.[9]

On the basis of some experience, Kierkegaard insisted that there is nothing more painful than being misunderstood. In fact, on his reading it was the impossibility of understanding Jesus's mission here on earth that set Christ's agony apart from the pain of others who have suffered for the truth.[10] Kierkegaard can often be caught sneering at those who cannot detect the pain that he takes such pride in being able to hide, yet the journals are rife with sighs of longing for human understanding and contact.

Like later depth psychologists, Kierkegaard recognized that the ego has its ways of deflecting painful affects. He perceived that depressives try to hide from their lack of feeling by sinking their self-consciousness in the world. This defense can take the form of debauchery. In psychoanalytic circles, it is common knowledge that certain types of depressives will eroticize their lives in an effort to stave off their depression. Better to dance with libidinal desire than to feel nothing. Kierkegaard's "The Seducer's Diary"[11] shows that he recognized this defensive strategy and his journals indicate that he saw himself as employing it in his own youth.[12]

In telling his writer's life story, Kierkegaard insists that the authorship was from the first to last a religious undertaking.[13] By his own account, it was also a radical defense against depression.[14] Kierkegaard understood his preternatural intellectual labors as an attempt to stay afloat from the preternatural depression that threatened to absorb him, much as it ultimately did his brother, who because of his depression, eventually resigned as Bishop of Seeland.

While there are lines in the pseudonymous authorship that would bring depression and despair close together,[15] there are strong indications that Kierkegaard saw a distinction between the state of depression and the activity of despair. For one, depression is a state or a mood whereas despair is an activity which only continues so long as the individual, however half consciously, wills that it continue. Anti-Climacus instructs us that it would be wrong to think of despair according to the medical model, that is as a fever, as a state which you passively suffer through. If despair did not engage the will it would not be the sin that Anti-Climacus insists it is. Kierkegaard does however use the disease model to describe depression. Indeed, he believes that depression is something that you can, as it were, be born into or catch by contagion. Kierkegaard describes his own melancholy in just this way, as an inheritance:

> An old man who himself was extremely melancholy... gets a son in his old age who inherits all this melancholy...[16]

The identity of the heir to the throne of sorrow is transparent. In another note, Kierkegaard leaves no doubt about his view of the etiology of depression:

> From the very beginning I have been in the power of a congenital mental depression. If I had been brought up in a more ordinary way—well, it stands to reason that I then would hardly have become so melancholy...[17]

In contrast to depression, Kierkegaard never talks about despair as though it were something you could contract by being around too many despairing people, or inherit as a child might inherit its mother's temperament.

The Sickness unto Death makes it plain that there are forms of despair which do not involve mental anguish. Indeed, Anti-Climacus, the pseudonymous author of this lapidary text, observes that happiness is despair's greatest hiding place.[18] While the depressed individual may, *a la* Kierkegaard himself, try and succeed at appearing happy, he is not happy. A person who is in fact happy is *eo ipso* not depressed. It is not, however, unusual for a happy person to be in despair. For another point of contrast, whereas depression always involves sadness, despair is not accompanied by a unique set of emotions. A walk through the psychospiritual portrait gallery presented in *The Sickness unto Death* will suffice to show that Kierkegaard believes despair to be compatible with both the blues and feeling in the pink.

No less than Nietzsche, Kierkegaard was a virulent critic of practical wisdom. The practical wisdom of *fin de siècle* America says that it would be a contradiction for someone to assert that he was depressed but in fine spiritual fettle. Kierkegaard contradicts this piece of practical wisdom. In a journal entry from 1846 that must be reckoned the axis of this chapter, Kierkegaard records the following signature self-observation:

> I am in the profoundest sense an unhappy individuality, riveted from the beginning to one or another suffering bordering on madness, a suffering which must have its deeper basis in a misrelation between my mind and body, for (and this is the remarkable thing as well as my infinite encouragement) it has no relation to my spirit, which on the contrary, because of the tension between my mind and body, has perhaps gained an uncommon resiliency.[19]

Clearly, the suffering to which Kierkegaard is riveted from the beginning and which he surmises to be a qualification of his particular mind/body relation is his melancholy. And yet in the above passage, he seems to be claiming that this psychological disorder (depression) is not to be confused with a spiritual malady. After all, he affirms that the misrelation between his mind and body has no relation to his spirit. We have here the distinction, effaced in our own age, between a psychological and spiritual disorder. In *The Sickness unto Death* and elsewhere we are told that a human being is not a simple synthesis between mind and body. Instead, "the self is a relation which relates to itself, or that in the relation which is relating to itself."[20] The simple and automatic relation between mind and body give rise to psychological states, but the spirit or self emerges in the way that we interpret and relate ourselves to those states. In that sense, the spirit is a kind of second order phenomenon.

To return to the journal entry from 1846, Kierkegaard notes that it is remarkable that the misrelation between his mind and body has not affected his spirit. In other words, his depression could in fact have become despair. The process by which depression becomes a sickness, not of the psyche but of the self, is not a passive one. In the first movement of the *Sickness Unto Death* Anti-Climacus sheds some light on his creator's diary and on the connection between depression and despair. Commenting on a case of depression, Kierkegaard's slightly abstracted doctor of the soul writes that the despairing depressive, "sees quite clearly that this depression etc. is of no great significance—but precisely that fact, that it neither has nor acquires any great significance, is despair."[21] It is not the psychological suffering itself that is the spiritual problem (despair) but rather being oblivious to the fact that the suffering has spiritual significance. As though he had been through that cast of mind, Kierkegaard writes, "The most dreadful thing that can happen to a man is that he becomes ludicrous in the essentials, that the substance of his feelings is drivel."[22] Though there are different internal paths from depression to despair, the depressive who sees no significance in his forlorn state, that is, who regards his sadness as a kind of fever, i.e., as drivel, has now developed a spiritual affliction to add to his psychological ills. Anyone who has had to trek through the inner tundra knows very well that the black sun can easily eclipse the very sense that suffering has a meaning, but it is primarily when the depressive throws up his hands and imagines that he is on some random rack that he has entered into the sin of despair.

Depression becomes despair by virtue of the way that the depressive individual relates himself to his depression. When a person who is suffering physical pain loses the ability to keep any of himself outside that pain, we say that he is in poor spirits. Likewise, when someone in agony is able to reach through the physical suffering and care about others, we say that he is in good spirits. The individual who is physically ill and in good spirits is able to avoid having his psychological life defined by his illness. Kierkegaard's journal entry suggests that a person who is psychologically tormented has some sway in the way that he relates himself to his psychological agony. The person who collapses and defines himself in terms of his depression, or the person who finds the wrong meaning in his depression, say, that it is proof that there is no merciful God, has of his own accord, slipped into despair.

For Kierkegaard, finding meaning in your depression is in effect grasping for the spiritual significance in your psychological suffering. In the edifying coda to the *Concept of Anxiety* ("Anxiety

as Saving through Faith"),[23] Vigilius Haufniensis instructs us on
how to sit for the spiritual instruction that only anxiety can offer.
In his better days, or some would say his worse, Kierkegaard
understood his depression to be a spiritual teacher. In the following jotting, Kierkegaard thanks Governance and his depression
for his understanding of the category of "the single individual":

> But who am I, then? Am I some devil of a fellow who has
> understood this from the beginning and has had the personal
> capacity to maintain it in my daily life? Far from it. I have been
> helped. By what? By a frightful melancholic depression, a
> thorn in the flesh. I am a severe melancholic who has the good
> fortune and the virtuosity to be able to conceal it, and for that
> I have struggled. But Governance holds me in my depression.
> Meanwhile I come to a greater and greater understanding of
> the idea and know indescribable contentment and sheer joy—
> but always with the aid of torment which keeps me within
> bounds.[24]

Kierkegaard took more advanced lessons from his depression.
For a Christian, there is no higher perfection than needing God,
the more intense the need the better.[25] And what, more than
inexplicable suffering, can make a person turn to God for help? It
is better, infinitely better, to understand feelingly how badly you
need God than it is to be psychologically well adjusted relative to
a community that Kierkegaard literally saw as a madhouse. Like
almost all psychological states, depression, according to
Kierkegaard, is dialectical—it can be reasonably taken one way or
the other. On the one hand, depression has crushed the breast-
bone of many a person's faith. Inexplicable and crippling sorrow
can be misunderstood to mean that existence is a slaughterhouse
without a director. On the other, seemingly entangled in himself
and feeling as though he can do nothing on his own, the
depressive is especially well positioned to grasp the fact of his
absolute dependence upon God.

According to Kierkegaard's self-interpretation, his depression
helped him to eschew the despair of forgetting about God.
Kierkegaard's identification with his father was both extensive
and deep. Both the *Journals* and his posthumously published
Point of View As an Author[26] suggest a special bond between father

and son around their shared melancholy. In the same year that he published the *Sickness unto Death*, Kierkegaard registers this strange debt of gratitude:

> I am indebted to my father for everything from the very beginning. Melancholy as he was, when he saw me melancholy, he appealed to me: Be sure you really love Jesus.[27]

While Kierkegaard was not beyond building questionable monuments to his father, this remark, made with reference to his own depression, seems to have functioned as the keystone of Kierkegaard's religious life. Kierkegaard frequently quipped that he loved and was attached to his innate sorrow or melancholy. While this kind of attachment was for him a temptation, he understood his heavy mindedness as making it virtually impossible for him to float off into the fantastic, which for a person with his mythopoeic imagination, stood as no small danger. To echo his words, Kierkegaard understood his depression as keeping him "within bonds" and always mindful of God. Kierkegaard writes:

> Yet it is an indescribable blessing to me that I was mentally depressed as I was. If I had been a naturally happy person— and then experienced what I experienced as an author, I believe a man necessarily would have gone mad.[28]

Once again, Kierkegaard repeatedly moans that the depression that he has inherited from his physical and spiritual father has placed him outside the household of humanity, condemned to human misery. And yet repugnant as it rings, there is he says one thing that he has never prayed to God for, namely, the removal of his thorn in the flesh. Very late in his dwindling days, Kierkegaard confesses:

> I dared to pray about everything, even the most foolhardy things, with the exception of one thing, release from a deep suffering that I had undergone from my earliest years but which I interpreted to to be part of my relationship with God.[29]

The notion that depression could be one of God's gifts is for the present age a hard saying. At times Kierkegaard seems to specialize in hard sayings. Indeed, amongst Kierkegaard scholars, many of whom are quietly offended by Kierkegaard's Christianity, there is an ongoing question as how to remove the gem of wisdom from the gangue of Kierkegaard's pietistic faith. So far as the present age is concerned, what does it matter if Kierkegaard draws a distinction between despair and depression if in fact this distinction rests upon the assumptions of a faith that have been politely put to bed? Or again, of what use is the distinction that Kierkegaard draws between psychological and spiritual disorders if in fact this distinction rests upon ontological assumptions which only the neurotic and/or half-witted are willing to make? Perhaps an edolcorated understanding of Kierkegaard's anthropology would claim that spirit has to do with the way that we relate ourselves to our immediate psychological lives as opposed to the psychological immediacy itself. To apply this bowdlerizing schema, the depressed but spiritually healthy individual understands that he is depressed but he does not see his life as defined by his depression. For instance, one of the most harrowing symptoms of depression is that it can pull the plug on feelings that are very much connected with our sense of identity. A depressed mother may at times seem to herself to feel nothing for her child. But to follow our secularized version of Kierkegaard's distinction, depressed as she may be, she can remain free of despair by remembering that she is depressed but does not really lack the love she may cease to feel. Once again, she does not surrender her identity to her illness. For Kierkegaard, the pitfalls leading from depression to despair always involve a misinterpretation of one's depression. Most commonly, the depressive who ends up despairing does so by coming to believe that he is only passively related to his depression, that he can, as it were, do absolutely nothing about the way he feels or acts. No doubt, the melancholic individual who is also in despair would regard the belief that he has some choice over the way he relates himself to his depression as a fantasy perhaps reminiscent of old Christian fantasies. So far as he is concerned, his understanding of his depression must be a facet of his depression. Kierkegaard, however, begs to differ in that he urges us to believe that the life of the spirit is something over and above our mental/emotional lives.

For those who cannot bear the rub of Kierkegaard's invocations to faith, a secularized version of the essence of Kierkegaard's understanding of despair might amount to the idea that the depressed and despairing individual gives up on himself. Appropriately enough, the English "despair" is related to the French "*desespoir*" indicating the negation of "*espoir*" or hope.[30] As previously noted, it used to be that despair was thought to involve actively pushing away hope relative to God, thinking, however passively or aggressively, that God could not or would not help. Instead of believing that for God all things are possible, including the possibility of healing his depression, the depressive in despair does not even try to trust that God is good and merciful and will make things right. Though he might be reluctant to acknowledge it, the despairing individual tries to murder such hopes as "God will help me through this." The author of the *Sickness unto Death* is unequivocal, the belief that God is dead is itself the deepest despair,[31] and yet for a culture which may be well along in the process of talking itself out of any serious belief in a personal God, it may be more accurate to say that despair occurs when the individual makes a point of no longer having hopes in or for himself. The most common form of despair considered from this angle might well be that of the individual who has fallen into the deep sleep of firmly believing that it has become impossible for him to change to any serious degree. Someone who fits in this category might, for example, have a moment wherein he wishes that he could be a warmer and more concerned friend, but in response to the ray of that longing, the despairing individual fists his soul and reminds himself that he is just not a warm and outgoing individual and, for that matter, never will be.

The present age is one with a natural propensity for translating relational ideas such as forgiveness into individual matters. There are, for instance, many people today who act as though their real task in forgiveness is not repentance but rather learning to forgive themselves. The idea that the transition from depression to despair is really a matter, not of giving up on God, but rather of giving up on oneself would certainly be consistent with this individualistic turn. Kierkegaard would no doubt regard the suggestion of taking God out of the formula for despair as an

intensely despairing way of understanding despair. As Kierkegaard would have it, the transition from depression to despair is
one of making oneself, perhaps angrily, perhaps pridefully, deaf
to God. And yet, so long as the depressive continues to listen for
the religious significance of the perturbations of his psyche, he can
avoid despair. It is not uncommon to hear depression described
as "hell on earth," and yet for Kierkegaard, it is as we have seen
entirely possible that a person could live in such a hell and still be
in robust spiritual condition. It is in fact entirely possible that he
saw both himself and the man he seemed to revere above all
others, his father, as psychologically disturbed and yet more than
less free of the despair that he found so pervasive in the era that
he called "the present age."

NOTES

[1] See the motto to Søren Kierkegaard's Concept *of Anxiety*, trans. Reidar
Thomte (Princeton: Princeton University Press, 1980), 3 (IV 274).
(Note: following every Hong edition page reference is the page
reference of the quote or section from the Danish 1st edition or the
Papirer.)

[2] I am here borrowing the term "sacred order" from Philip Rieff.

[3] Kierkegaard, *Concept of Anxiety* 121 (IV 389).

[4] See for example Vincent McCarthy's *The Phenomenology of Moods*
(The Hague: Martinus Nijhoff, 1978) and Kresten Nordentoft's
Kierkegaard's Psychology, trans. Bruce Kirmmse (Pittsburgh: Univer-
sity of Pittsburgh Press, 1978).

[5] It is evident from Kierkegaard's *Journals and Papers* that Kierkegaard
identified his thorn in the flesh with his depression. Consider 5:391
entry 6025 (VIII[1] A 205 *n.d.*, 1847), 6:153 entry 6396 (X[1] A 322
n.d., 1849), and 6:340 entry 6659 (X[3] A 310 *n.d.*, 1850)in *Søren
Kierkegaard's Journals and Papers*, ed. and trans. Howard and Edna
Hong, assist. by G. Malantschuk, 7 volumes. (Bloomington: Indiana
University Press, 1967). Henceforth, the *Journals and Papers* will be
referred to as *JP*, followed by volume number: page number and
entry number. Again, consider the parenthetical following that
references the quote's place in the *Papirer*.

[6] Kierkegaard uses two Danish terms to refer to depression, namely,
tungsindighed and *melancholi*. Vincent McCarthy argues that
tungsindhed which could be roughly translated as heavy mindedness
has deeper and more broody connotations than *melancholi*. See

McCarthy's *Phenomenology of Moods*, pp. 54-57. Abrahim Kahn disagrees, arguing that the two terms are synonymous in Kierkegaard's writings. See Kahn's "Melancholy, Irony, and Kierkegaard," *International Journal for Philosophy of Religion* 17 (1985): 67-85.

[7] *JP* 5:69 entry 5141 (I A 161 *n.d.*, 1836).

[8] For a signal example of this theme, consider the first page of Kierkegaard's most popular book, *Either/Or*, trans. Howard and Edna Hong, 2 volumes (Princeton: Princeton University Press, 1987). The text begins, "It may be times have occurred to you, dear reader, to doubt somewhat the accuracy of that familiar philosophical thesis that the outer is the inner and the inner is the outer" (3 (I v)).

[9] *JP* 5:389 entry 6620 (VIII^1 A 179 *n.d.*, 1847).

[10] See Kierkegaard's *Practice in Christianity*, trans. Howard and Edna Hong (Princeton: Princeton University Press, 1991), 136-137 (XII 127-128).

[11] Kierkegaard, *Either/Or, Volume 1* 301-445 (I 275-412).

[12] *JP* 5: 446-447 entry 6135 (VIII^1 A 650 *n.d.*, 1848).

[13] Søren Kierkegaard, *The Point of View*, trans. Howard and Edna Hong (Princeton: Princeton University Press, 1998), 23 (XIII 517).

[14] *JP* 5: 334-336 entry 5913 (VII^1 A 126 *n.d.*, 1846), 6: 475 entry 6840 (X^5 A 105 March 28, 1853).

[15] Consider, for example, the Judge's letters to 'A' in the second volume of *Either/Or*.

[16] *JP* 5: 334 entry 5913 (VII^1 A 126 *n.d.*, 1846).

[17] JP 6: 306 entry 6603 (X^2 A 619 *n.d.*, 1850).

[18] Søren Kierkegaard, *Sickness Unto Death*, trans. Alastair Hannay (London: Penguin Press, 1989), 55.

[19] *JP* 5: 334 entry 5913 (VII^1 A 127 *n.d.*, 1846).

[20] Kierkegaard, *The Sickness Unto Death* 43 (XI).

[21] Kierkegaard, *The Sickness Unto Death* 54 (XI).

[22] *JP* 4: 37 entry 3894 (IV A 166 *n.d.*, 1843-44).

[23] Concerning the spiritual instruction contained in this chapter, see my essay, "Anxiety in the *Concept of Anxiety*," in The *Cambridge Companion to Kierkegaard* , eds. A. Hannay and G. Marino (London: Cambridge University Press, 1998), 308-328.

[24] *JP* 6: entry 6659 (X^3 A 310 *n.d.*, 1850).

[25] See Søren Kierkegaard's *Eighteen Upbuilding Discourses*, trans. Howard and Edna Hong (Princeton: Princeton University Press, 1990), 297-326 (V 81-105).

[26] Kierkegaard, The *Point of View* 79 ff (XIII 564ff).

[27] *JP* 6: 12 entry 6164 (IX A 68 *n.d.*, 1848).

[28] *JP* 6: entry 6603 (X^2 A619 n.d.; 1850).

[29] *JP* 6: entry 6837 (X^5 A72 n.d. 1853).

[30] I am indebted for this observation to Vincent McCarthy. See his *Phenomenology of Moods*, p. 85-86.

[31] Kierkegaard, *The Sickness Unto Death* 158ff.

Bibliography

Works in Danish

Breve og Aktstykker vedrorende Søren Kierkegaard. Ed. Niels Thulstrup. 2 vols. Copenhagen: Munksgaard, 1953-4.

Samlede Werker. Ed. A. B. Drachmann, J. L. Heiberg, and H. 0. Lange. 3rd ed. 20 vols. Copenhagen: Gyldendalske Boghandel, 1962. 4th ed. forthcoming.

Søren Kierkegaards Papirer. Ed. P. A. Heiberg, V. Kuhr, and E. Torsting. 16 vols. in 25 tomes. 2nd ed., edited by N. Thulstrup, with an Index by N. J. Cappelorn. Copenhagen: Gyldendal, 1968-78.

English Translations

Hannay

Either/Or: A Fragment of Life. Trans. Alastair Hannay. Harmondsworth: Penguin Press, 1992.

Fear and Trembling. Trans. Alastair Hannay. Harmondsworth: Penguin Press, 1985.

Papers and Journals: A Selection. Trans. Alastair Hannay. Harmondsworth: Penguin Press, 1996.

The Sickness unto Death. Trans. Alastair Hannay. Harmondsworth: Penguin Press, 1989.

Hong

Journals and Papers. 7 vols. Ed. and trans. Howard V. Hong and Edna H. Hong, assisted by Gregor Malantschuk. Bloomington and Indianapolis: Indiana University Press, 1967-78.

Kierkegaard's Writings. Ed. and trans. Howard V. Hong, Edna H. Hong, Henrik Rosenmeier, Reidar Thomte, et al. 26 vols. projected

(20 vols. published as of August 19971. Princeton: Princeton University Press, 1978.

Volume I Early Polemical Writings: From the Papers of One Still Living; Articles from Student Days; The Battle between the Old and the New Cellars [1990)

Volume 2 *The Concept of Irony; Schelling Lecture Notes* (1989)

Volume 3 *Either/Or 1* (1987)

Volume 4 *Eitherl/Or 11* (1987)

Volume 5 *Eighteen Upbuilding Discourses* (1990)

Volume 6 *Fear and Trembling; Repetition* (1983)

Volume 7 *Philosophical Fragments; Johannes Climacus* (1985)

Volume 8 *The Concept of Anxiety* (1980)

Volume 9 *Prefaces* 1998

Volume 10 *Three Discourses on Imagined Occasions* (1993)

Volume 11 *Stages on Life's Way* (1988)

Volume 12 *Concluding Unscientific Postscript* (2 volumes; 1992)

Volume 13 *The Corsair Affair* (1982)

Volume 14 *Two Ages* (1978)

Volume 15 *Upbuilding Discourses in Various Spirits* (1993)

Volume 16 *Works of Love* (1995)

Volume 17 *Christian Discourses; Crisis [and a Crisis] in the Life of an Actress* (1997)

Volume 18 *Without Authority; The Lily in the Field and the Bird of the Air, Two Ethical-Religious Essays; Three Discourses at the Communion on Fridays; An Upbuilding Discourse; Two Discourses at the Communion on Fridays* (1997)

Volume 19 *The Sickness unto Death* (1980)

Volume 20 *Practice in Christianity* (1991)

Volume 21 *For Self-Examination; Judge for Yourself* (1990)

Volume 22 *The Point of View: The Point of View for My Work as an Author; Armed Neutrality; On My Work as an Author* (1998)

Volume 23 *The Moment and Late Writings; Articles from Faedrelandet; The Moment; This Must Be Said, So Let It Be Said; Christ's Judgement on Official Christianity; The Changelessness of God* (1998)

Volume 24 *The Book on Adler* (1998)

Volume 25 *Kierkegaard: Letters and Documents* (1978)

Volume 26 *Cumulative Index* (2000)

Other

Attack upon "Christendom" 1854-1855. Trans. Walter Lowrie. Princeton: Princeton University Press, 1968.

Christian Discourses. Trans. Walter Lowrie. London and New York: Oxford University Press, 1940.

The Concept of Dread. Trans. Walter Lowrie. Princeton: Princeton University Press, 1957.

Concluding Unscientific Postscript. Trans. David F. Swenson and Walter Lowrie. Princeton: Princeton University Press, 1968.

The Crisis [and a Crisis] in the Life of an Actress. Trans. Stephen Crites. New York: Harper and Row, 1967.

For Self-Examination and Judge for Yourselves. Trans. Walter Lowrie. Princeton: Princeton University Press, 1944.

The Journals of Søren Kierkegaard. Ed. and trans. Alexander Dru. London: Oxford University Press, 195 1.

Kierkegaard's Attack upon "Christendom. " Trans. Walter Lowrie. Princeton: Princeton University Press, 1944.

On Authority and Revelation, The Book on Adler. Trans. Walter Lowrie. Princeton: Princeton University Press, 1955.

Philosophical Fragments. Trans. David F. Swenson and Howard V. Hong. Princeton: Princeton University Press, 1962.

Prefaces: Light Reading for Certain Classes as the Occasion May Require, by Nicolaus Notabene. Ed. and trans. William McDonald. Tallahassee: Florida State University Press, 1989.

The Point of View for My Work as an Author: A Report to History. Trans. Walter Lowrie. London and New York: Oxford University Press, 1939; rev. ed., edited by B. Nelson, New York: Harper and Row, 1962.

The Present Age. Trans. Alexander Dru. London: Collins, 1963.

Works of Love. Trans. Howard V. Hong. New York: Harper and Row, 1962.

Books on Kierkegaard

Adorno, Theodor W. *Kierkegaard: Construction of the Aesthetic.* Ed. and trans. Robert Hullot Kentor. Minneapolis: University of Minnesota Press, 1989.

Agacinski, Sylviane. *Aparté: Conceptions and Deaths of Søren Kierkegaard.* Trans. Kevin Newmark. Tallahassee: Florida State University Press, 1988.

Beabout, Gregory R. *Freedom and Its Misuses: Kierkegaard on Anxiety and Despair.* Milwaukee: Marquette University Press, 1996.

Bell Richard H., ed. *The Grammar of the Heart: Thinking with Kierkegaard and Wittgenstein. New Essays in Moral Philosophy and Theology.* San Francisco: Harper and Row, 1988.

Bertung, Birgit, ed. *Kierkegaard: Poet of Existence. Kierkegaard Conferences.* Copenhagen: C. A. Reitzel Boghandel, 1989.

Bigelow, Pat. *Kierkegaard and the Problem of Writing.* Tallahassee: Florida State University Press, 1987.

————. *The Cunning, The Cunning of Being.* Tallahassee: Florida State University Press, 1991.

Brandt, Frithiof. *Den Unge Søren Kierkegaard.* Copenhagen: Levin og Munksgaard, 1939.

Brandt, Frithiof, and Else Rammel. *Kierkegaard og pengene.* Copenhagen: Levin og Munksgaard, 1935.

Bretall, Robert, ed. *A Kierkegaard Anthology.* New York: The Modem Library, 1959.

Cappelørn, Niels Jørgen, and Hermann Deuser, eds. *Kierkegaard Studiesl Yearbook* 1996. Berlin and New York: Walter de Gruyter, 1996.

Collins, James. *The Mind of Kierkegaard.* Princeton: Princeton University Press, 1983.

Come, Arnold B. *Kierkegaard as Humanist: Discovering My Self.* Montreal and Buffalo: McGill-Queen's University Press, 1995.

————. *Trendelenberg's Influence on Kierkegaard's Modal Categories.* Montreal: Inter Editions, 1991.

Connell, George B. To *Be One Thing: Personal Unity in Kierkegaard's Thought.* Macon, Ga.: Mercer University Press, 1985.

Connell, George B., and C. Stephen Evans, eds. *Foundations of Kierkegaard's Vision of Community.* Atlantic Highlands, N.J.: Humanities Press International, 1992.

Creegan, Charles L. *Wittgenstein and Kierkegaard: Religion, Individuality, and Philosophical Method.* London and New York: Routledge, 1989.

Crites, Stephen. *In the Twilight of Christendom: Hegel vs. Kierkegaard on Faith and History.* Camersbury, Pa.: American Academy of Religion, 1972.

Croxall, Thomas H. *Kierkegaard Studies.* London: Lutterworth Press, 1948.

Derrida, Jacques. *The Gift of Death.* Trans. David Wills. Chicago: University of Chicago Press, 1995.

Dewey, Bradley R. *The New Obedience: Kierkegaard on Imitating Christ.* Foreword by Paul L. Holmer. Washington and Cleveland: Corpus, 1968.

Diem, Hermann. *Kierkegaard's Dialectic of Existence.* Trans. Harold Knight. London: Oliver and Boyd, 1959.

Dunning, Stephen N. *Kierkegaard's Dialectic of Inwardness: A Structural Analysis of the Theory of Stages.* Princeton: Princeton University Press, 1985.

Dupré, Louis. *Kierkegaard as Theologian: The Dialectic of Christian Existence.* New York: Sheed and Ward, 1963.

Elrod, John W. *Being and Existence in Kierkegaard's Psenodonymous Works.* Princeton: Princeton University Press, 1975.

Emmanuel, Steven M. *Kierkegaard and the Concept of Revelation.* Albany: State University of New York Press, 1996.

Evans, C. Stephen. *Kierkegaard's "Fragments" and "Postscript": The Religious Philosophy of Johannes Climacus.* Atlantic Highlands, N.J.: Humanities Press International, 1983.

———. *Passionate Reason: Making Sense of Kierkegaard's Philosophical Fragments.* Bloomington and Indianapolis: Indiana University Press, 1992.

———. *Søren Kierkegaard's Christian Psychology: Insight for Counseling and Pastoral Care.* Grand Rapids, Mich.: Zondervan Publishing House, 1990.

Fendt, Gene. *Is Hamlet a Religious Drama? An Essay on a Question in Kierkegaard.* Milwaukee: Marquette University Press, 1998.

Fenger, Henning. *Kierkegaard: The Myths and Their Origins.* Trans. George C. Schoolfield. New Haven: Yale University Press, 1980.

Fenves, Peter. *Chatter: Language and History in Kierkegaard.* Stanford: Stanford University Press, 1993.

Ferguson, Harvie. *Melancholy and the Critique of Modernity: Søren Kierkegaard's Religious Psychology.* London and New York: Routledge, 1995.

Ferreira, M. Jamie. *Transforming Vision: Imagination and Will in Kierkegaardian Faith.* Oxford: Clarendon Press, 1991.

Fowler, James W. *Stages of Faith: The Psychology of Human Development and the Quest for Meaning.* San Francisco: Harper and Row, 1981.

Gardiner, Patrick. *Kierkegaard.* Oxford Past Masters. Oxford and New York: Oxford University Press, 1988.

Garff, Joakim. *"Den Sovnlose" Kierkegaard.* Copenhagen: C. A. Reitzels Boghandel, 1995.

———. *SAK: Søren Aabye Kierkegaard: en biografi,* Copenhagen, GAD 2000.

Golomb, Jacob. *In Search of Authenticity: From Kierkegaard to Camus.* London and New York: Routledge and Kegan Paul, 1995.

Gouwens, David J. *Kierkegaard's Dialectic of the Imagination.* New York: Peter Lang, 1989.

———. *Kierkegaard as a Religious Thinker.* Cambridge University Press, 1996.

Green, Ronald M. *Kierkegaard and Kant: The Hidden Debt.* Albany: State University of New York Press, 1992.

Grøn, Arne. *Begrebet angst hos Søren Kierkegaard.* Copenhagen: Gyldendal, 1993.

Hannay, Alastair. *Kierkegaard. The Arguments of the Philosophers.* Ed. Ted Honderich. London and New York: Routledge and Kegan Paul, 1982; rev. ed. (Routledge), 1991.

———. *Kierkegaard: A Biography.* Cambridge: Cambridge University Press, 2001.

Hannay, Alastair and Gordon Marino (eds.). *The Cambridge Companion to Kierkegaard.* Cambridge: Cambridge University Press, 1997.

Hendriksen, Aage. *Kierkegaard's Romaner.* Copenhagen: Glydendal, 1954.

Holmer, Paul L. *The Grammar of Faith.* San Francisco: Harper and Row, 1978.

Johnson, Howard A., and Niels Thulstrup, eds. *A Kierkegaard Critique.* New York: Harper and Brothers, 1962.

Khan, Abrahim H. *Salighed as Happiness? Kierkegaard on the Concept Salighed.* Waterloo, Ont.: Wilfrid Laurier University Press, 1985.

King, G. Heath. *Existence, Thought, Style: Perspectives of a Primary Relation Portrayed through the Work of Søren Kierkegaard.* Milwaukee: Marquette University Press, 1996.

Kirmmse, Bruce. *Encounters with Kierkegaard.* Princeton: Princeton University Press, 1996.

———. *Kierkegaard in Golden Age Denmark.* Bloomington and Indianapolis: Indiana University Press, 1990.

Law, David R. *Kierkegaard as Negative Theologian.* Oxford: Clarendon Press, 1993.

Lebowitz, Naomi. *Kierkegaard: A Life of Allegory.* Baton Rouge and London: Louisiana State University Press, 1985.

Lindstrom, Valter. *Stadiemas Teologie, en Kierkegaard Studie.* Lund: Haakon Ohlsons, 1943.

Lorentzen, Jamie. *Kierkegaard's Metaphors.* Macon: Mercer University Press, 2001.

Lowrie, Walter. *Kierkegaard.* London and New York: Oxford University Press, 1938.

————. *A Short Life of Kierkegaard.* Princeton: Princeton University Press, 1942.

McCarthy, Vincent A. *The Phenomenology of Moods in Kierkegaard.* The Hague and Boston: Martinus Nijhoff, 1978.

MacIntyre, Alasdair. *After Virtue.* South Bend, Ind.: University of Notre Dame Press, 1981.

Mackey, Louis. *Kierkegaard: A Kind of Poet.* Philadelphia: University of Pennsylvania Press, 1971.

————. *Points of View: Readings of Kierkegaard.* Tallahassee: Florida State University Press, 1986.

Maheu, Rene for UNESCO, ed. *Kierkegaard Vivant.* Paris: Gallimard, Collection Id6es, 1966.

Malantschuk, Gregor. *Kierkegaard's Thought.* Ed. and trans. Howard V. Hong and Edna H. Hong. Princeton: Princeton University Press, 1971.

Matustìk, Martin J., and Merold Westphal, eds. *Kierkegaard in Post-Modernity.* Bloomington and Indianapolis: Indiana University Press, 1995.

McKinnon, Alastair, ed. *Kierkegaard: Resources and Results.* Waterloo, Ont.: Wilfrid Laurier University Press, 1982.

Minear, Paul, and Paul S. Morimoto. *Kierkegaard and the Bible: An Index.* Princeton: Princeton Theological Seminary, 1953.

Mooney, Edward F. *Knights of Faith and Resignation: Reading Kierkegaard's Fear and Trembling.* Albany: State University of New York Press, 1991.

————. *Selves in Discord and Resolve: Kierkegaard's Moral-Religious Psychology from Either/Or to Sickness unto Death.* New York and London: Routledge, 1996.

Muller, Paul. *Kierkegaard's Works of Love: Christian Ethics and the Maieutic Ideal.* Trans. C. Stephen Evans and Jan Evans. Copenhagen: C. A. Reitzel Boghandel, 1993.

Nielsen, H. A. *Where the Passion Is: A Reading of Kierkegaard's Philosophical Fragments.* Tallahassee: Florida State University Press, 1983.

Nordentoft, Kresten. *Hvad Siger Brand Majoren? Kierkegaards Opgor med sin Samtid* Copenhagen: G. E. C. Gad, 1973.

————. *Kierkegaard's Psychology.* Trans. Bruce Kirmmse. Pittsburgh: University of Pittsburgh Press, 1978.

Pattison, George. *Kierkegaard.-The Aesthetic and the Religious: From the Magic Theatre to the Crucifixion of the Image.* New York: St. Martin's Press, 1992.

————. ed. *Kierkegaard on Art and Communication.* New York: St. Martin's Press, 1992.

Perkins, Robert L., ed. *International Kierkegaard Commentary:* The Concept of Anxiety. Macon, Ga.: Mercer University Press, 1985.

——. *International Kierkegaard Commentary:* Concluding Unscientific Postscript. Macon, Ga.: Mercer University Press, 1997.

——. *International Kierkegaard Commentary:* The Corsair Affair. Macon, Ga.: Mercer University Press, 1990.

——. *International Kierkegaard Commentary:* Either/Or. Macon, Ga.: Mercer University Press, 1995.

——. *International Kierkegaard Commentary:* Fear and Trembling and Repetition. Macon, Ga.: Mercer University Press, 1993.

——. *International Kierkegaard Commentary:* Philosophical Fragments and Johannes Climacus. Macon, Ga.: Mercer University Press, 1994.

——. *International Kierkegaard Commentary:* Two Ages. Macon, Ga.: Mercer University Press, 1984.

——. *International Kierkegaard Commentary:* Kierkegaard's Fear and Trembling: Critical Appraisals. Tuscaloosa: University of Alabama Press, 1981.

Pojman, Louis. *The Logic of Subjectivity: Kierkegaard's Philosophy of Religion.* Tuscaloosa: University of Alabama Press, 1984.

Poole, Roger. *Kierkegaard: The Indirect Communication.* Charlottesville: University Press of Virginia, 1993.

Poole, Roger, and Henrik Stangerup, eds. *The Laughter Is On My Side: An Imaginative: Introduction to Kierkegaard.* Princeton: Princeton University Press, 1989.

Roberts, Robert C. *Faith, Reason and History: Rethinking Kierkegaard's Philosophical Fragments.* Macon, Ga.: Mercer University Press, 1986.

Rosas, L. Joseph. *Scripture in the Thought of Søren Kierkegaard.* Nashville, Tenn.: Broadman and Holman, 1994.

Rudd, Anthony. *Kierkegaard and the Limits of the Ethical.* Oxford: Clarendon Press, 1993.

Shestov, Lev. *Kierkegaard and the Existentialist Philosophy.* Trans. E. Hewitt. Athens: Ohio University Press, 1969.

Slok, Johannes. *Kierkegaard-humanismens teenker.* Copenhagen: C. A. Reitzel Boghandel, 1978.

——. *Da Kierkegaard tav: Fraforfatterskab til kirkegstorm.* Copenhagen: C. A. Reitzel Boghandel, 1980.

Smith, Joseph H., ed. *Kierkegaard's Truth: The Disclosure of the Self. Vol. 5 of Psychiatry and he Humanities.* New Haven: Yale University Press, 1981.

Smyth, John Vignaux. *A Question of Eros: Irony in Sterne, Kierkegaard, and Barthes.* Tallahassee: Florida State University Press, 1989.

Spiegel, Shalom. *The Last Trial.* New York: Pantheon Books, 1967.

Stott, Michelle. *Behind the Mask: Kierkegaard's Pseudonymic Treatment of Lessing in the Concluding Unscientific Postscript.* Lewisburg, Pa.: Bucknell University Press, 1993.

Swenson, David F. *Something about Kierkegaard.* Minneapolis, Minn.: Augsburg Publishing House, 1941; 2nd ed., rev. and enl., 1945.

Tanner, John S. *Anxiety in Eden: A Kierkegaardian Reading of Paradise Lost.* New York and Oxford: Oxford University Press, 1992.

Taylor Mark C. *Kierkegaard's Pseudonymous Authorship: A Study of Time and the Self.* Princeton: Princeton University Press, 1975.

———. *Journeys to Selfhood: Hegel and Kierkegaard.* Berkeley and Los Angeles: University of California Press, 1980.

Theunissen, Michael. *Der Begriff Verzweiflung. Korrekturen an Kierkegaard.* Frankfurt am Main: Suhrkamp, 1993.

Thomas J. Heywood. *Subjectivity and Paradox.* Oxford: Basil Blackwell, 1957.

Thompson, Josiah. *Kierkegaard.* New York: Alfred A. Knopf, 1973.

———. *The Lonely Labyrinth: Kierkegaard's Pseudonymous Works.* Carbondale: Southern Illinois University Press, 1967.

———. ed. *Kierkegaard: A Collection of Critical Essays.* New York: Doubleday, 1972.

Thomte, Reider. *Kierkegaard's Philosophy of Religion.* Princeton: Princeton University Press, 1949.

Thulstrup, Niels. *Commentary on Kierkegaard's Concluding Unscientific Postscript, with a New Introduction.* Trans. Robert J. Widenmann. Princeton: Princeton University Press, 1984.

———. *Kierkegaard's Relation to Hegel.* Trans. George L. Stengren. Princeton: Princeton University Press, 1980.

Thulstrup, Niels, and Marie Mikulovd Thulstrup, eds. *Bibliotheca Kierkegaardiana.* 16 vols. Copenhagen: C. A. Reitzel Boghandel, 1978.

Wahl, Jean. Etudes Kierkegaardiennes. Paris: Fernand Aubier, editions Montaigne, 1938; 2nd ed., J. Vrin, 1949.

Walker, Jeremy D. B. *Kierkegaard: The Descent into God.* Kingston and Montreal: McGill–Queen's University Press, 1985.

———. *To Will One Thing: Reflections on Kierkegaard's "Purity of Heart"* Montreal and London: McGill–Queen's University Press, 1972.

Walsh, Sylvia. *Living Poetically: Kierkegaard's Existential Aesthetics.* University Park: The Pennsylvania State University Press, 1994.

Weston, Michael. *Kierkegaard and Modem Continental Philosophy: An Introduction.* London and New York: Routledge, 1994.

Westphal, Merold. *Becoming a Self: A Reading of Kierkegaard's Concluding Unscientific Postscript.* West Lafayette, Ind.: Purdue University Press, 1996.

———. *Kierkegaard's Critique of Reason and Society.* University Park: The Pennsylvania State University Press, 1991.

Wisdo, David. *The Life of Irony and the Ethics of Belief.* Albany: State University of New York Press, 1993.

Wyschogrod, Michael. *Kierkegaard and Heidegger: The Ontology of Existence.* New York: Humanities Press International, 1954.

INDEX

abstract thought, 33
anxiety, 41, 89, 98, 104-105, 109-110
Aristotle, 19, 31, 51, 64, 78, 88
The Concept of Anxiety, 89, 104, 110

continuity, 23-24, 27, 32, 49-50, 64, 66

death, 5, 7-8, 14-15, 17, 36, 55, 59-63, 65-69, 71-75, 77-81, 84, 93, 97-98, 102-103, 106, 108, 110-111
depression, 5, 15, 99-109, 111
despair, 5, 15, 48, 50-51, 99-105, 107-109, 111

Either/Or, 27, 44-47, 51, 58-60, 100, 110
ethics, 5, 8, 14, 43, 45-47, 49, 51, 53, 55, 57, 59, 84, 87-90, 92, 95, 97

faith, 5, 8, 14, 18, 24, 29, 31-41, 48, 51, 55-57, 64-65, 67-73, 79, 105, 107-108
fanaticism, 5, 8, 14, 29, 31-35, 37, 39, 41
Fear and Trembling, 37, 58, 67, 74
Freud, 5, 7-8, 15, 35, 40, 52, 77-81, 83, 85-95, 97-98

God, 14, 30-32, 35, 37-39, 56-57, 62, 65, 67-68, 70-72, 77, 85, 89, 99, 104-106, 108-109
Green, 59, 98

Hall, 8, 61-64, 67, 69-70, 72
Hegel, 18-19

immortality, 65-67, 72, 74

Johannes Climacus, 19, 25-27, 31, 39, 41, 47

madness, 5, 8, 29-33, 35, 37, 39, 41, 71, 84, 103
MacIntyre, 14, 43-49, 51-54, 56-60
melancholy, 100-103, 106, 110
morality, 44, 51, 55, 59, 88, 91, 93

objectivity, 14, 18-21, 33, 41, 64

Philosophical Fragments, 23, 39, 41, 46
psychoanalysis, 79-80, 98

reason, 5, 8, 14, 24, 34-36, 43, 45, 47, 49-55, 57, 59, 63, 65, 78, 84, 86, 91, 98, 102
resurrection, 63, 67, 73
Rieff, 3, 5, 7-9, 91, 109

self, 24, 32, 47-48, 52, 74, 91, 94, 103

The Sickness unto Death, 74, 93, 102-103, 106, 108, 110-111

spirit, 7, 30, 33, 36, 58, 93, 100, 103, 107

subjectivity, 29-30, 33, 36, 38, 40, 71

suicide, 5, 14, 17-19, 21, 23-25, 27, 32, 64

Two Ages, 25

Watkin, 73, 74

Works of Love, 8, 11-13, 15, 60

AUTHOR BIOGRAPHY

Gordon Marino took his bachelor of arts from Columbia University, his masters degree in philosophy from the University of Pennsylvania, and his doctorate from the University of Chicago, Committee on Social Thought. He is associate professor of philosophy and curator of the Hong/Kierkegaard Library at St. Olaf College. Marino co-edited the *Cambridge Companion to Kierkegaard* 1998. His essays on culture have appeared in the *Atlantic Monthly, Christian Century, Commonweal,* and many other periodicals.